CDL

Study Guide

2023-2024

BY

Chase Davis

CONTENTS

THE GUIDE TO CDL CERTIFICATION

1. To drive large vehicles intended for businesses or organizations, also known as Commercial Motor Vehicles or CMVs, you must have a CDL or Commercial Driver's License. This includes vehicles such as dump trucks, segmented busses, box trucks and others that require a CDL.

2. Since driving large commercial vehicles requires more technical skills than driving a small personal vehicle, obtaining an advanced driver's license means that you have completed the necessary training to safely and successfully drive a CMV.

3. If you are interested in a career as a truck driver, school bus driver, or operating other large vehicles, you may need to obtain a CDL before you are qualified for the job. While the specific requirements and regulations for obtaining a CDL may vary from state to state, this is a general guide on what a CDL is and how you can obtain one.

Forms of Licenses for Commercial Drivers

Commercial Driver's Licenses (CDL) come in three classifications: Class A, Class B and Class C. The type of CDL you need depends on the weight, function and capabilities of the vehicle you will be driving. Check the state website and job descriptions to determine which classification you need for your job.

When deciding which CDL to earn, consider the differences in preparation, experience, and vehicle requirements for each class. Start by determining the type of vehicle you want to drive, as this will determine the CDL you need to practice for. Here is an overview of each CDL class and which one might be right for you:

CDL Class A

The most common CDL is Class A and is required for the operation of any number of vehicles with a gross vehicle weight rating (GVWR) of 26,001 pounds or more, provided the GVWR of the towed vehicle is more than 10,000 pounds. The GVWR is the maximum weight a vehicle may carry. In most states, drivers with this license may drive any vehicle with two or more axles and a semitrailer or trailer. A Class A CDL is the more comprehensive CDL and authorizes driving vehicles commonly referred to as big rigs or 18-wheelers.

With a Class A CDL, you can also drive some Class B and C vehicles, depending on your endorsements. Examples of vehicles you can drive with a Class A license include livestock trucks, tractor-trailers, and passenger vans. A Class A CDL is the right choice if you are seeking employment as a licensed truck driver.

CDL Class A Training

Training for the Class A CDL may vary by program. It may include hands-on practice and behind-the-wheel training, vehicle maintenance, training on federal and state regulations, and other elements that teach students how to safely drive and operate a Class A vehicle. For drivers interested in operating a variety of commercial vehicles, the Class A CDL is a great option. The New England Tractor Trailer Training School (NETTS) offers a variety of Class A CDL training courses for drivers of all experience levels.

CDL Class B

The Class B CDL is intended for the operation of a single vehicle with a GVWR of 26,001 pounds or more and a vehicle towing another vehicle not exceeding 10,000 pounds. Depending on your endorsements, you may also be able to operate some Class C vehicles. Large passenger busses, dump trucks, and box trucks are examples of vehicles you can drive with a Class B license.

CDL Class B Training

Preparation for a Class B CDL usually consists of a combination of classroom instruction and driver training. Classes may vary depending on the curriculum, but may include general knowledge, training specifications, vehicle maneuvers, driving report writing, test planning, range, and on-road driving practice. Additional courses and training may include vehicle inspections, railroad crossings, freight hauling, general CDL, and vehicle awareness. The NETTTS offers a Class B Commercial Heavy Straight Truck Training (CDLB 80) licensing program that includes 80 hours of classroom and behind-the-wheel instruction.

Class A or B: Automatic vs. Manual

When obtaining your Class A or B CDL, it is important to consider the type of transmission you are practicing and applying for. If you are practicing with an automatic vehicle and the CDL driving test requires a manual transmission, you may not have the skills necessary to pass the test. It is also important that you know the types of vehicle transmissions used in the sector or position you are interested in applying for. If you get a CDL with an automatic transmission, you will only be trained to drive vehicles with automatic transmissions, which may reduce your chances of getting a manual transmission job.

Class C CDL

A Class C CDL is for the operation of a single vehicle with a GVWR of 26,001 pounds or more and other CMVs carrying 16 or more passengers (including the driver) or materials classified as hazardous under the Hazardous Materials Transportation Act.

Endorsements in the CDL

A CDL classification may not be sufficient for driving certain types of commercial vehicles. You may also need to acquire endorsements, which are essentially certificates that demonstrate your competency in driving a particular type of vehicle. Additional permits may be required to drive vehicles such as double or triple tractor-trailers, school busses, passenger vehicles carrying 16 or more passengers, hazardous materials (Hazmat) carriers, and tankers. Even if endorsements are not required for a particular job, they can make you a more competitive applicant and potentially earn you a higher salary. Consider an endorsement as a way to demonstrate your highly specialized skills and abilities as a professional driver.Alongside any CDL, you can receive the following endorsements:

- Hazardous materials (H): Inspection needed.
- Tank vehicles (N): Test required.
- Passenger (P): Required examination and driving test.

- School bus (S): Required examination and driving test.
- Double or triple trailers (T): Required examination.
- Tank vehicle and dangerous materials (X): Required examination.

How to Obtain a CDL?

The process for obtaining a CDL varies depending on the state in which you live. Therefore, be sure to check the guidelines on your state's Department of Motor Vehicles (DMV) website. In Pennsylvania, for example, a CDL is required to drive a vehicle with 16 or more passengers, including the driver, a school bus carrying minors, or a vehicle carrying hazardous materials. In California, a CDL is required for anyone whose primary activity is driving a vehicle, whether or not it is a commercial vehicle.

While the specific requirements for obtaining a CDL can vary from state to state, there are some general steps you can take to prepare for the process. These include meeting age and health requirements, obtaining a learner's permit, attending a CDL training program, passing a written exam and skills test, and paying the required fees. It is important that you carefully follow the steps and requirements set forth by your state to ensure that you are qualified to drive commercial vehicles safely and legally.

1. It is important to know the age restrictions in your state if you are seeking a CDL. In some states, you can obtain a CDL as young as 18; in others, you must be at least 20 years old or older. In addition, some states allow drivers under 20 to drive commercial vehicles within their state as indicated on their license. If you apply for a CDL at 18, you may be required to complete a state-approved driver education program or take additional steps. It's best to check with your state's DMV to make sure you meet all the requirements.

2. Before taking the CDL driving test, you must obtain a Commercial Learner's Permit (CLP) to practice the skills required for the test. The requirements for obtaining a CLP vary from state to state, but generally you will need to provide some documentation, such as a clean driving record, proof of medical fitness to operate commercial vehicles, and payment of the appropriate fees. In addition, you will have to pass a written test prepared by your state. Once you receive your CLP, you can use it to practice maneuvers and skills described in your state's CDL manual, which will be assessed on the CDL skills test.

3. To prepare for the CDL driving test, you must first obtain a Commercial Learner's Permit (CLP), which allows you to practice the skills required for the test. The specific requirements for obtaining a CLP can vary by state, but generally you will need to provide documents such as a clean driving record and proof of medical fitness to drive commercial vehicles, and pay the

appropriate fees. In addition, you must pass a written test prepared by your state. Once you have your CLP, you can use it to practice the maneuvers and skills described in your state's CDL manual, which will be assessed on the CDL skills test.

Get all the endorsements you need. Make sure you have obtained the required CDL endorsements for the type of vehicle you will be driving. There is an additional fee for this and, depending on the endorsement, you may be required to take a written test and/or a driving test.

After you have completed all the required courses, exams, paperwork and fees, it is time to get your CDL. If you pass the final test, some states will issue your license in person, while others will mail it to you. Once you have your license, check it carefully for errors or necessary changes to make sure it is valid for driving on the road.

Jobs Which Usually Need a CDL

Jobs transporting people, materials and goods are essential to support a stable economy. If you have excellent driving skills and prefer to be behind the wheel than behind a desk, a job as a driver could be ideal for you. Here are just a few examples of careers that could be a good fit for you:

- **Delivery Driver:** Delivery drivers transport packages, groceries and other items from one place to another. In this job, you'll often drive a van or small truck and may have to lift heavy packages.
- **Bus Driver:** Bus drivers transport passengers on a variety of routes, including city busses, school busses, and charter busses. This job requires good communication skills, patience, and the ability to handle unexpected situations.
- **Truck Driver:** Truck drivers transport goods and materials over long distances. This job requires specialized training and a commercial driver's license (CDL), as well as the ability to handle large, heavy vehicles.

There are many other types of driving jobs, including cab, ride-sharing, chauffeur, and specialized drivers for companies such as car rental agencies and limousine services. Regardless of your skills and preferences, there may be a driver job that is a perfect fit for you.

If you are interested in a career on the road instead of behind a desk, training for a Class A commercial driver's license (CDL) might be a good choice for you. Since 1986, a CDL has been required to drive certain types of vehicles, such as semi-trucks, semi-trailers and busses. Having a CDL makes you more marketable to potential employers, but some companies require new drivers to complete a certain number of ride-along hours to learn routes and loading protocols by shadowing an experienced truck driver. After you gain experience, you may even be able to start your own trucking company.

Driving a truck requires a higher level of expertise, experience and physical ability than driving a car. In an effort to improve highway safety and establish minimum requirements for a CDL, the federal government passed the Commercial Motor Vehicle Safety Act. However, each state issues its own CDLs and has its own specifications.

To learn more about Class A CDL standards in your state, or to learn more about CDL training and preparation for the driver's license exam, visit your state's Department of Motor Vehicles website.

If you are interested in a career as a truck driver, the median annual salary for truck and semi-truck drivers was $48,840 in May 2021, according to the U.S. Bureau of Labor Statistics, with the top 10% earning more than $72,140. However, salaries can vary depending on experience, location and type of vehicle driven. Bus drivers had a median annual wage of $44,140 in May 2021, with the top 10% earning more than $67,590. These figures can vary depending on the industry or company that employs the driver. If you are looking for CDL training in Pennsylvania, McCann School of Business and Technology can help you get the training you need. The school's CDL Training: Class A Tractor Trailer program offers instructors with real-world experience, full-size equipment, and opportunities for students to complete their CDL training by completing required driving hours.

UNDERSTANDING HOW A COMMERCIAL MOTOR VEHICLE (CMV) OPERATES WITH AIR BRAKES

In modern commercial vehicles, air brakes are one of the most important features. The air brake system on a commercial vehicle or semitrailer truck uses compressed air to force the brake pad into the brake drum, creating friction and slowing the wheel. While this may sound complicated, it's critical when you are braking a vehicle that can weigh up to 80,000 pounds. As long as the air brakes work efficiently and the driver knows how to operate them, the complexity is worth it. In addition, the company that owns and maintains the trucks needs to know what to look for to properly maintain the air brake system.

To ensure that air brakes are operating safely, it is important to understand how air brakes work.

Here is a simple description of how the air brake system works in a commercial vehicle:

The air brake system in a commercial vehicle works as follows: The air compressor pumps air into the air reservoirs, which are located under the vehicle or in reservoirs. The air is then forced through the brake air lines until it reaches the air brake. When the driver depresses the brake pedal on a commercial vehicle, the air pressure pushes out a rod that pushes the slack adjuster. The slack adjuster is used to calibrate the brake system and ensure that the internal spring mechanism is working properly. This spring mechanism creates the friction necessary to brake the vehicle.

Air flows through the nozzle into the air brake chamber, which then releases the spring to drive the "S-cam" The "S-cam" pushes the brake shoe lining against the brake drum, creating the friction and pressure necessary to slow the wheel. When the driver releases the brake pedal, the "S-cam" rotates back, allowing the spring to push the brake shoes away from the brake drum, removing the friction and braking effect.

The brake shoes will wear over time and due to the additional pressure created by the application of the brake pedal. It is recommended that commercial drivers and truck operators keep their brake shoes at a minimum thickness of one-quarter inch. Both the brake shoes and brake drum wear out over time and with excessive heat/wear, so it is necessary to test the air brake system periodically to ensure there are no faulty or unsafe components.

It is important that commercial vehicle drivers are trained in the use of the air brake system and perform regular inspections to ensure that the system is functioning properly. The Federal Motor Carrier Safety Administration (FMCSA) has issued regulations for the use and maintenance of air brakes on commercial vehicles to ensure their safety.

How Air Brakes Act

Imagine you are a new dockhand at a shabby trucking company, helping to load a huge semi-truck with cargo for the other coast. Suddenly, one of the captains orders you to move another truck out of the way to make room for a returning driver. However, you do not know how to drive such a large vehicle and hesitate. Nevertheless, the foreman assumes you can drive it and lets you.

You enter the cab of the truck, close the door and turn the key. You try to impress the supervisor, ignoring the fact that you do not have a truck driver's license. As the diesel engine starts, you are startled by a deafening beep and a flashing light on the dashboard. You start the engine, but the buzzer and flashing light continue to grab your attention.

Having driven a stick shift before, you assume you know how to operate the truck. Amidst the sensory overload, you step on the clutch, shift into what you think is low gear, and release the clutch. Instead of moving forward, the truck makes a loud bang, the engine stalls, and you are nearly thrown through the windshield.

You start the engine, realize you are in the wrong gear, and shift into what you think is the right gear. But inside the cabin, the buzzer and flashing lights are still causing chaos, and the emergency brake may still be engaged. You can not find any of the brake handles or levers typical of a vehicle, so you decide to let go of the clutch and try again.

Despite your efforts, you continue to have difficulty driving the truck and the foreman becomes increasingly frustrated. As he approaches you, you give up and flee the cab in shame. The book "Air Brake Planet" will explain how the air brake and its components work and how to maintain them. It will also clarify why you were unable to operate the truck and how this situation relates to the work of George Westinghouse.

Air Brake History

The use of air brake systems is critical to the safe operation of trains, busses and large trucks carrying heavy loads. Unlike hydraulic braking systems, which can leak brake fluid in the event of a leak, air brakes use compressed air to control the brakes. This prevents a potential disaster where a speeding vehicle relying on hydraulic brakes could become a deadly projectile if the brakes fail.

Before the development of air brakes, trains relied on a manual braking system in which the brakeman in each car applied a hand brake in response to the engineer's signal. This method was inefficient and dangerous. In 1869, George Westinghouse, an engineer in the railroad industry, developed the first three-valve air brake system for railroad cars. The system used an air compressor that fed air into the air tanks of each car through a brake line. Named for its three functions, the three-valve system worked in the opposite direction as the direct air brake system and provided improved safety and control for train braking.

The three-valve system developed by George Westinghouse for railcars performs three important functions: Charging, donning, and deflating. The system uses air pressure to release the brakes, and once air is pumped through the system, the brakes remain applied until the pressure is released. This is a critical safety feature, as a complete loss of air in the system would activate the brakes and stop the train. The three-valve system is still used today in air brake systems for on-road vehicles such as busses and semi-trucks. In the next section, you will learn more about how air brakes work in these vehicles.

Runaway Train Could Have Been Avoided

On June 27, 1988, a commuter train collided with a stationary train at the Gare de Lyon station in Paris, France. Fifty-six people were killed and 32 others were injured. The accident occurred after a series of errors resulted in the train's braking ability being drastically reduced. After a passenger accidentally pulled the emergency brake while disembarking, the engineer closed a brake valve thinking the device was equipped with an airlock. The train rolled freely after the air was removed from the system, but the remaining cars with the system loaded did not have enough braking power. The driver, in a panic, failed to activate the electric emergency braking system, and the train collided with a stopping train in the station. The death toll would have been much higher had it not been for a courageous engineer who stayed on the stationary train until it crashed to help evacuate the passengers (source: AP, National Geographic).

UNDERSTANDING OF BRAKES

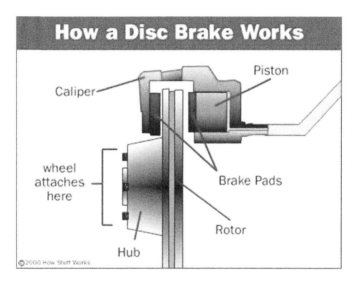

Let us take a look at how the brakes in your car work before we talk about air brakes in road vehicles. Anyone who has driven a car knows that when you hit the brake pedal on the concrete, the car slows down and eventually stops. But how can a 3,000-pound (1,361-kilogram) car traveling down the road at high speed stop with its feet?

Let us first discuss the different types of brakes and then examine the various components. One of the two systems is present in every rolling vehicle, including trains, semi-trucks, busses and cars. Hydraulic brakes, which are used in light-duty vehicles and passenger cars, use hydraulic fluid or oil to brake. In the next part, we'll take a closer look at air brakes, where the brakes are powered by air. Let us take a look at the distinctions.

In a hydraulic system, fluid is contained in a tank commonly referred to as the master cylinder. The fluid is pumped through brake hoses or lines onto pistons that are attached to each wheel when you press the brake pedal. These brake pistons either push against two brake shoes that expand in a brake drum and cause friction, or they push against a brake pad that holds onto a brake disk. Below are the parts of a hydraulic disk brake system.

- Brake reservoir: Include hydraulic fluid for brakes.
- Master cylinder: Machinery that pumps the fluid to the brake lines that run in the vehicle from the reservoir.
- Brake lines: Braided hoses of rubber or steel which run from the master cylinder to each brake caliper.
- Brake caliper: A steel housing that mounts a piston and brake pads on a brake rotor's fixed point.
- Brake piston: A circular rod that, when hydraulic fluid is fed from the master cylinder, stretches and pushes against a brake pad.
- Brake pad: A semi-metallic overlay of metal backing pad that grips the steel rotor.
- Brake rotor: A steel disk mounted on each wheel and hub that the pads grip to avoid the wheels' rotation.

Here's a look at how several of the components work inside a disc brake.

Before disk brakes, cars relied on drum brakes. The main mechanics were the same, but drum brakes used brake shoes that sat on a rotor in a drum attached to the hub. Because disk brakes are easier to cool and provide more surface area to attack, they increase braking power. Also, disk brakes are easier to remove brake dust, which forms as brake pads wear and reduces braking power, than drum brakes.

Now that we understand the basics of brakes in trains and vehicles, let us talk about large trucks and busses.

Components for Air Brakes in Trucks and Buses

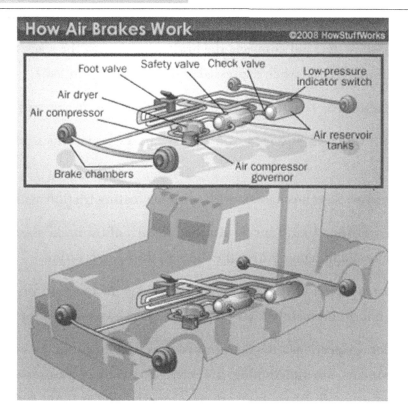

Air brake elements diagram.

The air brake systems most commonly used in trucks and busses are foundation brakes and operate in the same manner as in rail vehicles. Air accumulates in the brake tubes or air lines using the three-valve principle and releases the brakes. Virtually all road vehicles equipped with air brakes have a staged release system in which a partial increase in pressure determines the proportional release of the brakes.

In a truck or bus, the following components are exclusive to the foundation air brake system:

1. **Air compressor:** The air is pumped into storage tanks for use in the braking system.

2. **Air compressor governor:** Monitors the air compressor's cut-in and cut-out point to maintain a fixed amount of air in the tank or tanks.

3. **Air reservoir tanks:** Carry compressed or pressurized air for the braking system to use.

4. **Drain valves:** Release valves are used to drain the air in the air tanks while the car is not in operation.

5. **Foot valve (brake pedal):** Air is expelled from the reservoir tanks when depressed.

6. **Brake chambers:** Cylindrical container housing a slack adjuster shifting the mechanism of a diaphragm or cam.

7. **Pushpin:** A steel pin connects the brake chamber to the slack adjuster, similar to a piston. The brakes are released when depressed and applied if extended.

8. **Slack adjusters:** To adjust the brake shoes' distance, an arm ties the pushrod to the brake S-cam.

9. **Brake S-cam:** An S-shaped cam that separates brake shoes and drives them against the brake drum.

10. **Brake shoe:** Steel mechanism with a lining creating friction against the brake drum.

11. **Return spring:** A rigid spring attached to each of the brake shoes that, when not extended by the S-cam or diaphragm, returns the shoes to the open position.

Proper maintenance is critical for air brake systems to function properly and prevent brake failure. Here are some important maintenance steps for air brake systems:

1. **Regular inspections:** Regular inspections are essential to ensure that all air brake system components are functioning properly. These inspections should include looking for leaks, making sure all valves are working properly, and making sure the air compressor is working properly.

2. **Keep the system clean:** Dirt, oil, and other contaminants can damage air brake system components. Regularly clean the system and keep it free of debris to ensure proper function.

3. **Replace components as needed:** Like all mechanical systems, air brake components wear out over time. Regularly replace brake pads, brake shoes, and other components as needed to prevent failure.

4. **Check and maintain proper air pressure:** Air pressure is critical for air brake systems to function correctly. Ensure that the system is always pressurized to the correct level.

5. **Use the right air dryer:** Air dryers are an essential component of air brake systems, removing moisture from the compressed air. Make sure to use the right air dryer for your system, and change the desiccant as needed.

By following these maintenance steps, you can ensure that your air brake system remains functional and prevent brake failure.

What Is the Sound?

Have you ever thought about the strange sounds trucks and busses make when they come to a stop? The squealing sound is the sound of air escaping from the braking system after the brakes are applied, while the hissing sound comes from the automatic safety bypass valves that keep air pressure at the proper level. Since air is the key element in the operation of air brake systems, the compressor runs continuously, cycling on and off to fill the reservoirs with compressed air. When the compressor produces an excess of air, the valves open and produce a distinct hissing sound.

Air Brakes: Maintenance Preventative

When air brake systems are not properly maintained, it can lead to dangerous accidents. Each state in the United States has specific regulations for driving a vehicle with air brakes. To obtain a commercial driver's license, you must pass rigorous tests and adhere to strict maintenance guidelines. Before you hit the road, it's important to follow a few steps to ensure safety. For example, you should verify that the minimum operating pressure for a bus is not less than 85 psi and for a truck is not less than 100 psi. You should also make sure that it does not take more than two minutes to build up the air pressure from 85 psi to 100 psi at 600 to 900 rpm. Another important aspect is to verify that the compressor cutoff regulator pressure is correct, which should be between 120 psi and 135 psi, with a cut-in pressure of 20 psi to 25 psi below the cutoff pressure.

It is also important to watch for water in the air brake system, as air brake lines do not tolerate water well, especially in colder climates where it can freeze and cause wheels to lock up. Look for modern systems with automatic drain valves located in each air reservoir to avoid this problem. Worn air clutch seals can also cause air to leak, leading to compressor failure if the compressor is overloaded. Another byproduct of air brakes is brake sensitivity, which can lead to accidents, especially for inexperienced drivers. Air brake systems are designed for heavily loaded vehicles and can cause the rear wheels of trailers to lock up when empty, resulting in double skid marks on the highway.

For truck drivers, a clunk is one of the worst fears. It occurs when the rear end of the trailer comes up against the cab, and braking too hard can cause trucks to buckle easily in rain and snow. Most modern air brake systems have a dual mechanism, so two systems are available in case one fails. Anti-lock braking systems are also found in semi-trucks and work similarly to the ABS systems in passenger cars. Although air brake systems are reliable and effective, their size and the attention they require make them unsuitable for use in vehicles. Just look at a Peterbilt truck on the highway and you will notice the large tanks behind the fuel tanks.

Poor Maintenance Leads to Runaway Truck

In Plymouth Meeting, Pennsylvania, a tragic accident occurred on April 25, 1996, between a 1988 Mack cement truck and a small Subaru sedan. The cement truck was traveling down a steep ramp and approaching an intersection when its brakes failed. As a result, the truck drove through the intersection and collided with the Subaru, killing the driver. The National Transportation Safety Board investigated the accident and discovered several problems with the truck, including inverted brake lines and a secondary system failure. Due to these problems, the vehicle had only an estimated 17 to 21 percent of its total braking capacity, which ultimately led to the accident. Unfortunately, the driver was unaware of the brake failure, and proper maintenance could have prevented the incident.

Hazardous Materials Understanding, Handling, and Shipping

Handling hazardous materials is a very serious task because it has the potential for significant environmental and property damage, loss of productivity, and even injury or death. Regulations in this area are very strict, and the penalties for non-compliance are severe. It is critical that all workers involved are well trained and on the same page when it comes to safety.

Despite the challenges, it is possible to create a hazardous materials training program that not only ensures safety, but also improves productivity. In this guide, we'll give you a basic overview so you can ensure your hazardous materials training, storage and shipping practices meet current standards and regulations. While there is much more to learn, these tips will provide you with a solid foundation to build upon.

HAZARDOUS MATERIAL—AN INTRODUCTION

To ensure protection from hazardous substances, it is important to have a thorough understanding of the risks associated with each type of substance. To do this, you must study the wealth of information available on these substances, particularly the GHS or Internationally Harmonized Scheme for the Classification and Labeling of Chemicals. This system for classifying hazardous materials is used by carriers, shipping industry associations and government agencies around the world to determine the hazards of a particular category of cargo and how it should be handled.

It is also important to know that there is even more extensive knowledge about hazardous materials that you should also be familiar with. The U.S. Department of Transportation's Hazardous Materials Table provides a comprehensive list of all hazardous materials and their associated restrictions. This table is a detailed and specific guide to safely transporting hazardous materials, covering everything from storage to quantity to packaging and more.

Hazardous Products Educational Activities

Without the proper knowledge base, it is difficult for an employee to properly handle hazardous materials, which is why training is so important. According to the PHMSA Hazmat Training Handbook, there are five main types of training that any agency managing hazardous materials must conduct:

1. General awareness training to promote understanding of hazmat protection at the base level.

2. Function-specific training on any hazmat-related tasks they have to conduct with each employee.

3. Safety instruction on avoiding injuries, responding to emergencies, and developing a general safety culture.

4. Security awareness instruction on basic hazmat transportation safety procedures.

5. In-depth compliance training for workers with higher security duties on the basic aspects of the security policies.

PHMSA guidelines require businesses to maintain logs on their hazmat training program, including the forms of training that have been obtained by workers and how recently. Before starting work or within 90 days, workers must complete their training under direct supervision by a professional employee.

It's necessary to lay out the foundation of what you want to achieve first to get the best out of your employee training. When creating a hazmat training program, here are some important questions you might ask:

- What workers have job functions that include preparation for hazmat?
- In which hazmat courses do they need training?
- Are there workers currently employed with materials for which they have not been formally trained?
- What methods of hazmat transportation do you use?
- Have there been shifts in strategies, goods, leadership, or other areas that cause current workers to be retrained?
- How will you incorporate preparation into the onboarding phase, and how are you execute it for existing employees?

Answering these questions will help you make decisions about how to build your exercise program. It's time to start looking at training strategies until you clearly understand what you want the training program to accomplish.

PHMSA's Hazardous Materials Training Modules are one of the best training tools available for free. These online modules cover the basics of handling hazardous materials that every worker should know, including documentation, labeling, protection and more. They are not a comprehensive source of training, but they are a good place to start. PHMSA also offers a series of webinars and seminars throughout the year that provide detailed guidance on general and specific topics.

For more comprehensive training, you may need to contact a hazmat trainer who holds certifications from various organizations, such as the Department of Transportation (DOT), the International Maritime Association (IMO), and the International Air Transit Association (IATA). Fortunately, there are several organizations that offer solid, dedicated hazmat training programs, and many others that specialize in helping companies expand their offerings.

Various hazmat training courses, both in-person and online, are offered by companies like Infotrac and Lion Technology. Be sure the training program includes a schedule of when employees must recertify their training programs. Laws at DOT require recertification every three years for hazardous materials employees.

As you prepare your training program, it is also important that you are aware of some of the key principles that you need to include. Next, we will discuss some of the most commonly discussed aspects of hazmat training and some of the best practices your company should follow.

Practices for Hazardous Materials Handling

Proper handling of hazardous materials is critical to workplace safety, from the home to the warehouse or storage facility. To prevent accidents, it's important to include the following practices in your training program and follow them diligently when storing hazardous materials:

1. **Proper storage:** The hazardous materials should be stored in designated areas that are clearly marked and separate from other materials. They should be stored according to their compatibility and away from potential sources of ignition.

2. **Labeling:** All hazardous materials must be labeled properly and accurately, indicating the contents of the container, the associated hazards, and emergency response information.

3. **Handling and transportation:** When handling hazardous materials, appropriate personal protective equipment (PPE) should be worn, and any spills or leaks should be immediately cleaned up. During transportation, hazardous materials should be properly secured and labeled, and all regulations pertaining to their transport should be followed.

4. **Emergency response:** An emergency response plan should be in place in the event of an accident, including measures such as first aid, spill cleanup, and evacuation procedures.

By following these practices, you can ensure that hazardous materials are stored safely, reducing the risk of accidents and promoting a safe work environment.

When integrated into a comprehensive training program, these activities can provide a solid foundation for the safe storage of hazardous materials. For many companies, however, storage is only part of the equation, and it is transportation that presents the greatest challenge.

Transporting hazardous materials requires careful planning and execution to prevent accidents or spills. This includes properly labeling and securing materials for transport, ensuring compatibility with other transported goods, and complying with all relevant regulations and guidelines.

In addition, drivers must be properly trained and equipped to handle hazardous materials during transport. This includes using appropriate PPE, knowing what to do in an emergency, and knowing the proper procedures for loading and unloading hazardous materials.

Overall, transporting hazardous materials requires a high level of care and attention to detail to ensure that these materials are transported safely and securely to their destination. Combined with proper storage, these measures can significantly reduce the risk of accidents and help create a safe work environment for all employees involved in handling and transporting hazardous materials.

Hazardous Substance Shipping Activities

Transporting hazardous materials is a complex and challenging endeavor, and creating an effective training program can be especially difficult for those new to hazardous materials transportation. However, a solid foundation of knowledge is critical to safe transportation. This includes familiarizing yourself and your employees with the rules and regulations for transporting hazardous materials, such as the International Air Transit Association (IATA) Dangerous Goods Code, the International Maritime Hazardous Goods Code, Title 49 of the Code of Federal Regulations and the Emergency Response Guidebook.

To ensure your employees are equipped to handle dangerous goods, they should be trained to correctly complete the Dangerous Goods Shipper Declaration forms, which provide legal proof that dangerous goods have been properly declared. They should also be familiar with coordinating dangerous goods with the carriers used for shipping, taking into account variables such as the USPS dangerous goods table, DOT dangerous goods certification, and the specific dangerous goods transportation regulations of each carrier.

It is important to have all relevant codes available in your shipping facilities, either in digital or book form. In addition, personnel should be adequately trained and qualified to respond to emergencies involving hazardous materials, and the emergency response guide should be readily available.

Ultimately, safety comes first when handling hazardous materials, and there are no shortcuts or compromises. Best practices must be followed at every stage of operations, from training to transportation to storage. With accumulated knowledge from decades of safely transporting hazardous materials, there is always a right way to handle hazardous materials, and the only way is the right way.

The transportation of hazardous materials is an area where mistakes can have serious consequences, including injury, property damage and even death. However, with attention, coordination and patience, it is possible to transport these materials safely and efficiently. The safety of people, products and the company are all interrelated. That's why it's important that you use high-performance hazardous materials packaging that protects all three. To help you navigate the complex world of hazardous materials transportation, we have compiled a list of seven common mistakes you should avoid.

One of the most important aspects of safe and compliant hazardous materials transportation is proper labeling and declaration of goods. Transparency is essential, and all dangerous goods products must have the appropriate UN dangerous goods labels and/or dangerous goods placards describing the hazard class of the contents. These products must also be reported on the official shipper's declaration form to ensure that all hazardous materials personnel know what they are transporting and how to handle it.

It is also important to consider the differences in the means of transportation. Laws and regulations can differ significantly for some products and packaging methods when transported by surface or air freight. For example, cooling dry ice is subject to different regulations for each mode of transportation. Therefore, it's important to make sure you know what standards apply to your products, especially if you are working with a freight forwarder.

Another common mistake to avoid is not knowing the relevant laws for each hazardous material. Visit DOT for detailed tables of hazardous materials and the relevant regulations for each substance. Your company is required to comply with these regulations for everything it ships.

Assuming items are not labeled as hazardous can also lead to errors. There are many items classified as hazardous that the average consumer may not think of as such. Depending on the mode of transport and quantity, lithium-ion batteries, common medical specimens, fuel cell systems, genetically modified organisms and more may be classified as hazardous. When in doubt, do your homework and contact your shipper or carrier to ensure compliance.

Another mistake you should avoid is letting untrained employees handle hazardous materials. Employees must be properly qualified and trained, and structured preparation is no substitute for hands-on experience in hazardous materials transportation. Employees should demonstrate their competence under supervision before being allowed to handle hazardous materials on their own.

Another mistake to avoid is not following the packaging manufacturer's instructions exactly. Hazardous materials packaging is designed to comply with various regulations governing the transport of hazardous materials, and reputable suppliers of hazardous materials packaging provide clear instructions on how to use their packaging. Make sure employees using the packaging have easy access to and understand the instructions.

Assuming others would overlook mistakes is a common one you should avoid. It can be tempting to think that hazmat violations will not be noticed, but the U.S. government is cracking down on non-compliant hazmat shipments. The risk is never worth it, and even if you escape a fine, someone could get hurt.

Mistakes can happen, but in the hazmat transportation industry, it's important to minimize them. With the right practices, you and your employees can be more efficient in keeping everyone safe and ensuring a smooth supply chain by watching for common mistakes and taking precautions.

COMBINATION VEHICLES FOR CDL

How to Prepare for Inspection CDL Combination Vehicles

General Information

This study guide provides a brief overview of the essential information needed to drive combination vehicles, which are often hybrid vehicles used in the CDL exam. A combination vehicle is a tractor-trailer that is connected to one or more trailers, also known as a "semi" or "semi-truck" The connection is usually made with a fifth wheel and/or a conversion trailer. The fifth wheel, located in the center, makes the combination vehicle easier to maneuver, but can complicate tasks such as setup, driving, dashboard operation, braking and backing.

Significant Questions about the Safety

Ensuring safety is crucial when operating any commercial vehicle, but driving a hybrid vehicle such as a combination vehicle can be more challenging than operating a straight truck. There are several areas of concern that are unique to combination vehicles, so it is essential to understand and adhere to the safest practices while driving. Here are some significant questions to consider regarding safety when operating a combination vehicle:

1. Do you have the necessary training and experience to operate a combination vehicle safely?

2. Are you familiar with the unique features and controls of a combination vehicle, such as the fifth wheel, converter dolly, and air brake system?

3. Have you properly inspected the vehicle before starting your trip, including checking tires, brakes, lights, and coupling devices?

4. Do you understand the importance of weight distribution and how to properly load and secure cargo on a combination vehicle?

5. Are you aware of the potential challenges of turning, backing up, and braking a combination vehicle, and do you know how to handle these situations safely?

6. Have you considered the impact of weather and road conditions on driving a combination vehicle, and do you know how to adjust your driving accordingly?

7. Do you understand the importance of maintaining a safe following distance and checking blind spots when operating a combination vehicle?

8. Have you familiarized yourself with the relevant safety regulations and guidelines for operating a combination vehicle, and are you committed to following them at all times?

By asking these questions and taking the necessary steps to ensure safety, you can minimize the risks and operate a combination vehicle safely and efficiently.

Rollover Risk

When driving a mixed vehicle, the chance of rollover increases dramatically. To help reduce the threat:

- Always hold freight as close to the ground as possible.
- Use gentle steering. This is important because of the "crack-the-whip" effect that occurs when vehicles pull trailers.

   Hint: You could be on your written DMV test with the two facts above.

- Fast lane changes trigger rearward amplification.
- Even without overturning the tractor, it may overturn the trailer.
- The most likely to roll over is the rearmost trailer.

   Hint: You could be on your written DMV test with the two facts above.

Braking

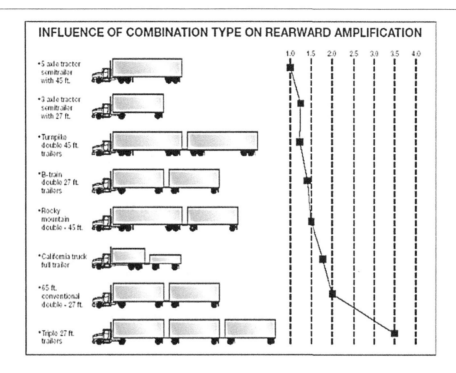

Some facts and advice you must need to know:

- It takes much longer to stop empty trucks than fully loaded trucks, and are at a higher risk of jackknifing.
- It takes much longer to stop bobtails (tractors with no trailers attached).
- Trucks with lightly loaded suspension systems have low traction, and the knife on the wheels and/or jack is more likely to lock.
- It takes longer to stop large vehicles than smaller vehicles.
- When driving a hybrid car, you still brake early.
- Keep mindful of your surroundings. Stop stopping the fear.
- Try to be mindful of what you see in your mirrors to escape jackknifing. A strong indication that your trailer is skidding can be seen in your mirrors. Release the brakes instantly if this happens and attempt to regain control of your car.

Railroad Tracks

- Railroad tracks, especially if you are towing trailers with low ground clearance, can cause problems for combination vehicles.
- Never stop on railroad tracks for any car.
- Never change gears when crossing railway routes.

Hint: You could be on your written DMV test with the two facts above.

Equipment which is particularly susceptible to getting stuck on elevated railroad tracks:

- Lowboy trailers.
- Car carriers.
- Moving vans.
- Trailers for possum-belly livestock.
- Single axle tractors that pull long trailers (especially if the landing gear of the trailer is arranged for a double axle tractor).

Hint: Your written DMV test might contain the information above.

- Get out of the vehicle and drive away from the tracks if your truck becomes stuck on railroad tracks. Support with contacts.

Note: The information below is possibly not part of your written DMV exam, but it is essential to know about the railway's safety.

A DOT sign identifies several public railroad crossings. DOT Signs are usually blue with white lettering. On the signs you will find an (800) number and a special DOT crossing number. This DOT number is the best way for the railroad to identify a particular grade crossing. There may also be the city name, street names, or other information. Call the (800) number and read the details on the sign. Call 911 if you cannot find a DOT placard (or the correct (800) number).

Near crossings, DOT placards are prominently located. There may be DOT placards attached to:

- A nearby shack for railroad equipment.
- The crossing process.
- The crossing arm.
- Cross buck pole (two X-shaped signs with the words "Railroad" and "Crossing").

Do not hesitate. As soon as possible, contact support.

When the wheels of a trailer lock, the trailer begins to swing. The trailer could reach another lane and eventually overturn the entire truck. If the trailer is light or unloaded, this is very likely.

Recovery from a skid on a trailer:

- Recognize the skid. Check your mirrors if you brake sharply.
- Get the brakes off. To regain wheel traction, release the brakes.
- The trailer will begin following the tractor again when the wheels grip again—braking resume.
- Do not use the trolley bar (hand brake for the trailer). The skid was triggered by trailer brakes, which can solve the problem by releasing the brakes.

Hint: Maybe this is for your written DMV exam.

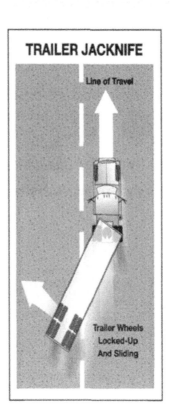

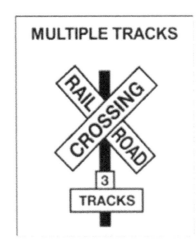

Turn Wide

When a vehicle travels in a straight line, all wheels follow the steering wheels. However, when the vehicle turns, the rear wheels take a different path, which is called "swerving" or "cheating" The reason is that each wheel takes a shortcut when turning. The rear wheels sheer the most, especially with long trailers.

To ensure safety when turning, steer the front wheels far enough to avoid any obstacles on the inside of the turn. However, avoid swinging too far and leaving a gap between the curb and your trailer, as this could allow other drivers to pass you on the right or get stuck between the rear of your trailer and the curb.

If you are unable to make the turn completely in your lane, you should pull out wide when you finish the turn (button hook) or before you start the turn (jug handle). In this way, you avoid potential hazards and can turn safely.

Hint: You might see this on your written DMV test.

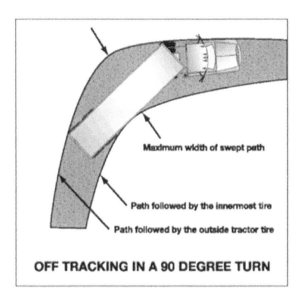

OFF TRACKING IN A 90 DEGREE TURN

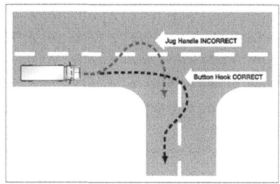

Backing Up

Reversing a combination vehicle can be a difficult task that requires caution and attention. To reverse safely, it is important to check your surroundings slowly and use both mirrors. If possible, have someone guide you when backing up. If you notice that the trailer is deviating from the intended path, correct it quickly by either turning the steering wheel or driving forward.

When reversing, try to keep the trailer in a straight line. If you need to maneuver the trailer to the driver's side, it is better to do so because you can see better from that side than from the passenger's side.

Hint: Your written DMV test might include these facts.

When reversing a combination vehicle, it is easier to use the driver's side mirrors than the passenger side mirrors. In addition, it may be helpful to roll down the driver's window and look over your shoulder. If necessary, it is recommended to stick your head out the window. It's better to have a little snow on you than to back into something.

Remember: It is important to use the "get out and look" technique (GOAL) when backing up with a combination vehicle. Even experienced drivers should use this technique to ensure they have a clear view of their surroundings and are aware of potential obstacles or hazards. Getting out of the cab and looking around the corner and behind the trailer can help you see blind spots or areas that are not visible in the mirrors. It is recommended that you get out and look several times, if necessary, to ensure that the reverse maneuver is performed safely.

Note: On the written DMV exam, you won't see the following bits of advice, but this is good advice for driving professionally.

When maneuvering your vehicle in a busy yard, such as backing up to a fence, it is important to keep your cool and not rush. Remember, GOAL (Get out and Look) and back up safely. Other drivers may be waiting for you to leave, but it is better to take your time and avoid an accident. If you notice that your truck is not in line with the door, do not proceed immediately. Wait until the other drivers start driving and then try again. This will help you avoid feeling rushed and distracted by the other drivers.

Note: The following bit of details about the written DMV test will not be visible.

Backing a trailer is challenging. You will spend approximately half your driving time at the truck driving school:

- Sustaining a trailer.
- Shifting a non-synchronized, manual gearbox.

Air Brakes Combination Vehicle

The information in this section assumes you have read the "Air Brakes Test" study guide already. Before reading this part, do so, or you will be confused.

Description of Details Contained in the "Air Brakes Test" Study Guide

The "Air Brakes Test" Study Guide explains the operation of:

- Trailer safety valve.
- Regulation of trailer air supply.

   Hint: This could be on your written DMV test.

- Air trailer tanks.
- Support for trucks, parking, and emergency braking.
- Anti-lock braking system (ABS)

Before taking the written DMV test for combination vehicles, check the material in our "Air Brakes Test" study guide.

Briefly, briefly:

- If the trailer breaks free or there is a major air leak in the trailer, the trailer safety valve cuts off the trailers air supply.
- The trailer air supply regulator is the red, eight-sided regulator knob on the truck dashboard that controls the trailer safety valve and, if the air pressure gets too low, will "pop out."
- In the rear of the vehicle, the Vehicle Air Tanks store pressurized air near where it will be needed. To trigger the trailer brakes, air from the tanks (controlled by the relay) is used.
- The three basic braking systems on modern tractors and trailers are trailer operation, parking, and emergency brakes.
- During hard braking, the ABS prevents wheels from locking up and increases vehicle stability. ABS does not reduce the interval between stops.
- Chocks should always be used while parking a trailer that has no spring brakes. The trailer could roll away if air leaked out of the trailer.

Hint: Maybe this is for your written DMV exam.

- There will be an ABS warning light on the trailer's left rear corner of the trailer is fitted with ABS (it is rarely seen on the trailer's left nose). This indicator is going to be yellow and called "ABS."

Hint: Maybe this is for your written DMV exam.

- In the driver-side mirror, the ABS indicator light can be seen and flash several times when the machine is started. This indicator light (if the ABS is working normally) would then turn off. If the ABS indicator light continues to flash (or is continuous "on"), your ABS has a problem; contact a mechanic.

Hint: Maybe this is for your written DMV exam.

Hand Valve Trailer

The trailer hand valve, also known as the "trolly valve" or "Johnson Bar," should only be used to control trailer brakes and not while the vehicle is in motion. This valve only affects the trailer brakes, and if you use it while driving, the trailer brakes may lock up, causing the trailer to skid or tip over. It is important to know that this information may be asked on the written driver's license test.

The foot brake applies both the trailer and tractor brakes, reducing the risk of skidding or jackknifing. Also, the trailer's hand valve should never be used for parking, as a leak in the air system could cause the brakes to release and the trailer to roll. Instead, use the parking brake or wheel chocks if the trailer does not have spring brakes.

Air Lines Trailer

There are two types of compressed air lines for trailers:

The "blue" service line, which is also called the "control line" or "signal line."

The "red" emergency line, which is also called the "supply line".

The service line, identified by its blue color, supplies air to the relay valves located near the brake cylinders. These valves control the vehicle's brakes using compressed air from the vehicle's air tanks. Both the trailer's foot and hand brake valves regulate the operating line, with higher pressure resulting in greater braking force.

The emergency air line, identified by its red color, serves two purposes. First, it fills the trailer's air tanks with air that powers the trailer brakes controlled by the relays. Second, it activates the emergency brakes. A loss of air pressure in the emergency brake line can cause the trailer's emergency brakes to suddenly activate. Note that the suspension system also uses air from the trailer air tanks to fill the air bellows, but this has nothing to do with the brakes.

Couplers for Hose (Gladhands)

Gladhands are air couplings that connect the tractor's air system to the trailer's air system. There are two types of gladhands: service and emergency, each color-coded and labeled. Before use, make sure all four rubber seals are clean and free of cracks. If the lines are not connected, the trailer air tanks will not charge and the brakes will remain locked. When not using the trailer, secure the tractor doors to the mock hitch or tie them together and hook them to the rear of the tractor to prevent them from being exposed to moisture and soil. Always test the trailer brakes before driving by applying the brakes and gently pulling against the trailer in low gear. It is advisable to carry extra Gladhand seals as they can easily break or get lost.

Shut-off Valves on Trailers and Converter Dollies

Shutoff valves are located on the back of trailers used to tow other trailers and on the back of converter dollies. Each trailer and dolly has two shutoff valves, one for "service" and one for "emergency" All shutoff valves must be open except for the two shutoff valves at the rear of the truck, which must be closed.

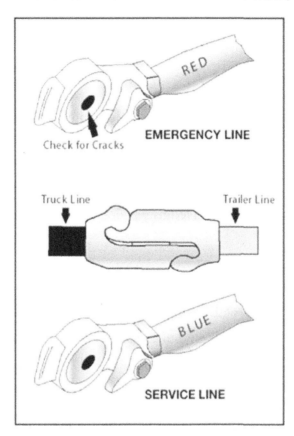

Hint: Your written DMV test could include the above facts.

Check the valves for shut-off:

- Set brakes or chock wheels for tractors.
- Charge the emergency line. (Press the red knob-trailer air supply control.)
- Supply the service line with air. (Use the handbrake lever for trailers.)
- Go to the rear portion of the rear trailer.
- Open the emergency line shut-off valve. You need to hear air escaping.
- Open the valve for the shut-off on the service line. You need to hear air escaping.
- Close the valve for shut-off.
- Brake parking package.

Hint: The steps above may be for your written DMV test.

Note: Shut-off valves are often referred to as cocks that are cut-out. Cocks are a type of valve that flips from fully open to fully closed at 90 degrees. Cocks are either 100 percent open or 100 percent locked, unlike normal valves that can be open, locked, or partly open/closed.

Uncoupled and Coupling

For safe driving, learning how to couple and uncouple a combination vehicle is important. Procedures vary from rig to rig, but standard steps are expected to be followed.

Coupling

With a total of 15 stages, the coupling is a lengthy process. These are the first six steps for coupling:

1. Fifth-wheel inspection:

- Test the damaged/missing components.
- Properly fixed to the frame, without any cracks.
- Greased plate. (Due to friction between the trailer and the tractor, an improperly greased plate may cause steering issues.)
- Correctly located fifth-wheel: plate tilted down toward the trailer, jaws open, handle unlocking (if equipped) in automatic position (ready to lock), kingpin (on the trailer) not bent or broken.

2. Area inspection and chock wheels:

- Zone clear around the vehicle.
- Chocked wheels (if the trailer is not fitted with spring brakes).
- Ensure that the cargo is secured.

3. Tractor-position:

- Place the tractor in front of the trailer immediately.
- Do not turn around at an angle under the trailer. The trailer could be moved sideways, and/or you could bend the landing gear.

4. Return slowly:

- Back before the trailer hits the fifth-wheel.
- Do not return to the trailer at this stage. Before slipping under the trailer, you need to get out and check the fifth-wheel and kingpin alignment.

5. A secure tractor:

- Set the brakes for parking.
- Place neutral transmission (or park, if fitted with an automatic transmission).

6. Trailer height check:

- Get out of the tractor and look at the trailer's fifth wheel and nose.
- If the tractor slips under the nose of the trailer, the trailer should be raised slightly.
- Ensure that the fifth wheel's rear does not strike the nose (front) of the trailer.
- Search the open end of the fifth-wheel for the kingpin to join.
- The kingpin could latch incorrectly if the trailer is too high. The jaws will attempt to cling to the kingpin's head.

  Hint: This may be in the written exam for the DMV.

- The kingpin could ride right over the plate of the fifth-wheel if the trailer is too big. The nose of the trailer could strike the back of the tractor cab.

  Hint: This may be in the written exam for the DMV.

These are the final ten steps for coupling:

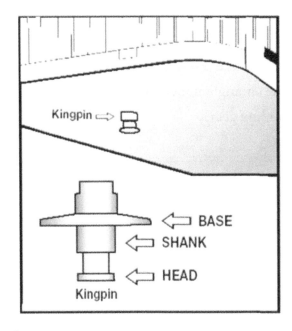

1. Air lines link to the trailer:

- Test the glad-hand gaskets. (They should be free of cracks and clean.)
- Link "Service" to "Service" and "Emergency" to "Emergency."
- Help air lines so that they are not pinched or crushed during the connection process.
- At this stage, do not attach electrical lines.

2. Supply the trailer with air:

- Charge trailer air tanks. (Press the trailer air supply control red knob.)
- Let us normalize the trailer air tanks.
- Trailer brakes are pressed and released, and regular brake operation sounds are listened to.
- Look for signs of massive air leakage from the gauges.
- Get the engine started.
- Watch the gauges until there is regular air pressure.

3. Lock the brakes on the trailer:

- Set trailer emergency/spring brakes. (Pull out the trailer air supply control, red knob.)

4. Back to the trailer:

- The lowest reverse gear is used.
- Back slowly under a trailer.
- Stop when the kingpin is locked ("click" is heard).

5. Security link search:

- Slowly lift the landing gear.
- Slightly pull the tractor forward (while the trailer brakes are still used).
- Movement check. (The tractor needs to "buck" slightly. The trailer does not move.)

6. Stable lorry:

- Position the neutral transmission (or park, if fitted with an automatic transmission).
- Set brakes for parking.
- Turn off the engine and bring your key with you.

7. Coupling Inspect:

- Make sure that there is no room or gap between the fifth wheel and the trailer's rim. (Get out and look. Use a torch.)
- Ensure the fifth-wheel is correctly positioned in the kingpin.
- Ensure that the fifth-wheel jaws are fully clamped on the kingpin shaft (not on the head of the kingpin).
- Ensure the locking lever is locked (if equipped).
- Inspection requires getting off the tractor, climbing under the trailer, and looking into the fifth-wheel jaws. If required, use a flashlight.

   Hint: This may be in the written exam for the DMV.

- There should be no gap between the trailer nose on the fifth-wheel plate and the underside.

   Hint: This may be for the written DMV test.

8. Attach and inspect the air lines with the electrical cable:

- Attach the electrical cord to the trailer's nose. (Typically, the electrical cord is green.)

- Look for signs of wear on electrical cables and air lines.
- Help electrical cords and air lines, so nothing while driving (including turning) would not be pinched or crushed.

9. Boost the support of the front trailer (landing gear):

- Completely lift the landing gear. (Don't run a trailer with only partially raised landing gear. On railroad tracks or rough terrain, partially raised landing gear will catch.)

Hint: This may be for the written DMV test.

- Protect the handle of the crank.
- Verify that the landing gear or trailer nose during driving/turning would not hit the tractor.
- Check the tractor tires do not strike trailer tires.

10. Remove and store wheel chocks for trailers:

- Chocks are removed (if used).
- Uncoupled

Here are the uncoupling steps:

1. Rig in place:

- Choose a suitable trailer landing spot.
- Ensure that the ground bears the weight of the trailer.
- Attach the tractor to the trailer. (At an angle; pulling out will damage the landing gear.)

2. Relieve tension on locking jaws:

- Trailer brakes lock. (Draw out the red knob of the trailer air supply control.)
- Relieve pressure by gently supporting the fifth-wheel jaws. (The tractor needs to "buck" slightly. The trailer does not move.)
- Set the parking brakes while pressing the tractor back into the cab.

3. Trailer wheels chock:

- Chock wheels (when the trailer does not have spring brakes).

4. Lower the gear for landing:

- When the trailer is clear, lower the gear until it hits the ground firmly.

- If the trailer is loaded, lower the gear until it reaches the ground firmly, then give the handle of the crank a few extra turns. (These extra turns will reduce the strain on the fifth wheel and jaws and make it easier for the next driver to pick up the trailer, making uncoupling easier.)

5. Disconnect the electrical cables and air lines:

- Disconnect air lines in the dummy coupler and put glad-hands.
- Disconnect the electrical cord and position the dummy coupler electrical connector.
- Make sure the air lines and electrical cords are supported when driving and will not be harmed.

Note: In an emergency, the glad-hands are built to fall apart, but they will "snap-together" and crash into the tractor cab. This may harm the tractor. By taking it apart without disconnecting it, the electrical cord would be weakened (or ruined).

- Disconnect and neatly store the air lines and electrical cord properly.

6. Unlock the wheel on the first:

- Unlock (if equipped) handle lock.
- Pull the handle on the unlock.

Warning: Be extra careful at this stage and keep your body away from the fifth wheel and watch for equipment movement. Expect the machinery to move, possibly in an unpredictable direction. The tractor or trailer could move as soon as the release handle is pulled. Do not place your body in the path of the damage. Be especially careful when uncoupling in tight spaces (or between trailers). Leave yourself a "way out".

7. Push the tractor slightly away from the trailer:

- Pull the fifth wheel out of the trailer below.
- Stop in case the landing gear collapses, with the frame under the trailer.

8. A secure tractor:

- Brake set for parking.
- Place the neutral transmission (or park, if fitted with an automatic transmission).

9. Trailer supports inspect:

- Landing gear search.
- Ensure that the ground supports the trailer.

10. Push the tractor straight out of the trailer:

- Unlock the brakes for parking.
- Drag the trailer forward and clear.

Combination Care Vehicle

When inspecting a combination vehicle, it is important to follow the traditional seven-step inspection process and inspect the coupling system areas (such as the lower and upper fifth wheels, the trailer air and electrical lines, and the sliding fifth wheel) and landing gear during the walk-around. In addition, the trailer's air brakes must be inspected as part of the air brake system inspection. This includes inspecting the air flow of all tractors, testing the tractor's safety valve, and testing the trailer's emergency and service brakes. Combination vehicles have various trailer brake control components, such as trailer air lines, hose couplings (gladhands), trailer air supply control, tractor safety valve, trailer air tanks, trailer manual valve, shutoff valves, trailer operation, parking and emergency braking. Therefore, it is important that you become familiar with all of these components before operating a rig.

Facts Bonus

You need to know-how:

- Test trailer service brakes.
- Test trailer emergency brake.
- Check the valve for tractor safety.
- Check the flow of air through all trailers (shut-off valve test).

The guidelines for conducting these tests are in this study guide and/or in our Air Brakes Research study guide.

Designed before 1975, converter dollies and trailers are not expected to have spring brakes like newer trailers; instead, they have emergency brakes.

The thing most often forgotten in pre-trip checks are driver's licenses and vehicle registrations. Before driving, make sure you have the trailer and tractor registration. The trailer registration is usually located in a waterproof container on the nose of the trailer.

THE CDL'S DOUBLES/TRIPLES TEST STUDY

1. How to Get Ready for the Doubles/Triples CDL Test

Before You Start

It is important that you review the Air Brakes Test and Combination Vehicles Test study guides before taking the DMV written test for Doubles/Triples. This is because the written tests are usually taken at the same time. Understanding the information in these study guides will help you better prepare for the doubles and triples test. Make sure you study and understand all the relevant information before taking the exam to increase your chances of passing.

General Information

This study guide contains the essential information you need to safely operate double or triple trailers. These combinations are connected with a converter dolly, a short trailer with a ring hitch on the front and a fifth wheel on the top. The dolly contains various components such as lights, air tanks, relays, wiring, brakes, ABS and electrical connections. When equipped with ABS, the dolly has a yellow indicator light on the left side.

It is important to know that the converter dolly has spring brakes, which may be asked about in your DMV written exam. However, very old converter dollies may not have such brakes, so when in doubt, it is best to use wheel chocks. Also, it's important to know that not all trailer combinations are allowed in every state. For example, triple trailers are not allowed in California, but they are allowed across the border in Nevada.

Helpful Illustrations

The general arrangement between the lead trailer (left) and the following trailer (right) for the converter dolly.

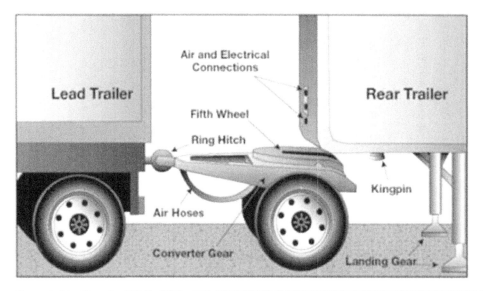

The Definitions

LCV: Longer Combination Vehicle.

Pup trailer: A 26 feet to 29 feet trailer commonly used in doubles and triples.

Safety Considerations for Double/Triple

Owing to their size and length, doubles and triples pose several special problems for drivers. Some of them are here:

Rollovers

Compared to single trailers, double and triple trailers are more prone to rollovers, especially the last trailer in the combination. Abrupt movements can cause the trailer to sway and result in a phenomenon known as "crack-the-whip" To prevent the trailer from tipping over, drive carefully around curves, maintain a steady speed, and apply the brakes in a timely manner.

Space Management

Double and triple trailers require more space and attention when maneuvering than single trailers. When turning or changing lanes, it is important to use caution and avoid colliding with curbs or other vehicles. Gradual speed adjustments and observation of traffic can help prevent overturning and loss of control. Lane changes should only be made with adequate space, as more axles can cause skidding or overturning. Choosing parking spaces that allow easy passage can also help prevent accidents. In bad weather, it is especially important to drive with extra caution.

Hook and Ring Hitch Pintle

Never cut the snap hook under a trailer when the dolly is under it. The weight of the trailer can (and almost certainly will) cause the ring hitch to fly up. This can be very dangerous.

Considerations of Inspection

During the regular seven-step inspection of double and triple trailers, you will need to remember a few extra things:

- The shut-off valves must be open at the rear of the front trailer(s), and the shut-off valves must be locked at the rear of the rear trailer(s). (All the valves, except the valves at the very rear of the vehicle, must be open.)
- Confirm that the drain valve of the convertor dolly air tank is closed.
- Ensure the support of the air lines and that the glad-hands are linked.
- Check that the spare tire is secured, the dolly's ring hitch is in place, the pintle hook is latched, the safety chains are secured, and the electrical cords secure their sockets.
- Additionally, always ensure that the lightest trailer is in the rear and the heaviest is in the front when filling a double/triple trailer.
- Converter dollies are like very short trailers (in many forms). Many of the sections are equivalent.
- The second and third trailer couplings are the same as double couplings.
- There are more brake elements. Double and triple brakes are the same as (or somewhat similar to) the brakes on a single combination vehicle. There are two or three trailers instead of one trailer and a dolly or two. The inspection method of doubles and triples is very close to the inspection of a regular combination vehicle. The measures are similar. It just takes longer.

Note: The procedure for checking a combination vehicle's shut-off valves (including doubles and triples) is found in the Combination Vehicles study guide.

Hint: Your written DMV test might contain that information.

Uncoupled and Coupling

Double Trailers

The steps are as follows for double trailers' coupling:

1. Secure the second trailer.
2. The converter dolly is positioned in front of the second trailer.
3. Pair the tractor and the first semi-trailer (standard procedure followed).
4. Connect the converter dolly (pintle hook and ring hitch) to the front trailer.
5. Connect the converter dolly to the rear (fifth-wheel) trailer.

Begin by lowering the second trailer's landing gear, then uncouple the rear trailer (at the fifth wheel) to disconnect the double trailer. By lowering the dolly's landing gear, loosening the safety chains, tightening the spring-loaded brakes or wheel chocks, loosening the snap hook, and pulling away from the dolly, the converter dolly will be uncoupled. Never loosen the snap hook under a trailer while the dolly is under it. The weight of the trailer will cause the ring hitch to be thrown up (this is almost certain). This can be very dangerous. Make sure the height of the trailer is correct. If the dolly is supported underneath, the trailer should be slightly raised. There should be no clearance between the top of the fifth wheel and the bottom of the trailer.

To secure a trailer from hitching, make sure the trailer is equipped with a spring brake and that there is no air in the emergency air line (red line) or:

- Set the emergency brakes by charging the emergency air line, filling the trailer air tank, then removing the air out of the emergency air line.
- Use chocks.

Hint: This information may be on your written DMV test.

Triple Trailer

As with double trailers, the steps for coupling triple trailers are the same, with the following extra steps:

1. Couple the second and third trailers.
2. Get the tractor uncoupled and pull away from the trailers.
3. Pair the tractor and the first semi-trailer (after the normal procedure).
4. Pair the tractors and the first semi-trailer to the second and third trailers.

5. Uncouple the third trailer by removing and uncoupling the dolly like you would for the double trailers.

THE CDL TANKER TEST STUDY

How to Prepare for the Test of CDL Tankers

General Information

The commercial driver's license (CDL) tanker test assesses drivers' ability to safely operate a tanker truck, which is a vehicle designed to transport liquids or gasses. Safety is a critical factor in evaluating drivers for the road, especially since tank trucks are large and very heavy. Because of their unique characteristics, tank trucks require different handling, maintenance, inspection and safety procedures compared to other commercial vehicles.

Do You Need an Endorsement for Tankers?

If you carry a liquid or liquid gas, you need a tanker endorsement:

- Where the capacity of any tank exceeds 119 gallons.
- Where the overall combined size of all the vehicle's tanks is 1,000 gallons or more.

It doesn't matter if hazmat is present in the tanks. It doesn't matter if the tanks are attached to the vehicle permanently or temporarily. If the tank(s) are over one (or both) caps, you need a tanker endorsement.

Exception for Flatbed

If the tank is empty, not equipped for transportation, and temporarily attached to a flatbed vehicle, the vehicle is not a tanker.

Exception for Commercial Learner's Permit (CLP)

You can run a tank vehicle if it is empty if you have a CLP with a tank endorsement. If the empty tank had already held hazmat, the tank must have been purged.

Inspection

Tankers are more complex compared to other types of commercial vehicles. This is mainly due to the special piping, valves, and conveyor systems required to transport the materials being carried. Before operating a tank truck, it is essential to know the specific procedures and safety measures required to inspect and control tank systems. Read the owner's manuals before starting such work.

Leaks Check

All inspections of commercial vehicles should include a check for leaks. The most obvious place to look for signs of leaks is in the field under the vehicle. Also inspect the frame and equipment under the frame for signs of leaking contents.

Check also:

- Intake/discharge ports and cut-off valves.
- Tank body (shell) free of leaks and dents.
- Valves (not leaking and incorrect position).
- Pipes (notably for joints and elbows).
- Hoses in good condition and properly stored.
- Locked and latched manhole covers (and/or sealed).
- The vents are clear, do not leak, and typically operate.
- Both covers and ports have gaskets and are closed.
- Tires in good condition (check for leaked material in "tire spray" and on tires).
- Equipment of special intent.

Some tankers are fitted with specialized equipment for service, protection, and emergency:

- Kits for vapor recovery.
- Cables grounding/bonding.

- Emergency equipment for the shutdown.
- Fire extinguishers built-in.
- Automatic system of fire suppression.
- Equipment for fire and protection.

Depending on what is carried in the tank, you could need additional equipment. It requires Personal Protective Equipment (PPE), special tank equipment, or specialized protective equipment. Find out what is needed, and be sure it's all working.

Unsafe Appliances

Do not use tanks that have leaks. You can be fined and/or dismissed. You might be in charge of cleaning up any spills. Never drive a vehicle with valves or manhole covers that are open.

Handling of Trucks

High Gravity Center and Risk of Rollover

The center of gravity of commercial vehicles is higher than that of a passenger car. For this reason, commercial vehicles have an increased risk of rollover. Tankers have one of the highest centers of gravity and a correspondingly high risk of rollover.

Surge

Tanker trucks have a high center of gravity and are also susceptible to what is called a "surge" A surge occurs when liquid in the tanks shifts and pushes the truck forward or backward. This can cause a truck to collide with a stationary vehicle or even be pushed into an intersection. On icy roads, a spill can be especially dangerous because it can cause the truck to roll over. Therefore, it is important to be familiar with how the truck handles, both in good and bad road conditions.

Bulkheads

Tankers with bulkheads are designed to mitigate the effects of wave action and improve sailing stability. By dividing the tank into smaller compartments, the surge is spread over several seconds, minimizing its impact on the ride. You can find out the number of smaller tanks and their respective volumes by inspecting the fittings or checking the owner's manual. It is important to know that one of the smaller tanks may have a slightly different volume, so the timing of the pressure surge will be different for each tank. When filling the tanks, it is important to distribute the weight evenly to avoid putting all the weight on the front or rear of the vehicle.

Baffles

Baffles are internal structures with holes in some tanks designed to reduce the effects of surge during travel by extending the time it takes for the liquid to slosh through the tank. Sloshing baffles look similar to bulkheads, but they do not divide the tank into smaller compartments. Instead, they are placed inside the tank and are designed to help control the surge from front to back. Although they can effectively reduce the effects of surge on handling, bulkheads typically do not have lateral control. It is important that drivers understand the specific structure of the tank they are operating and how the surge baffles or other features can affect driving and safety.

Surge

Tanker trucks have a high center of gravity and are also susceptible to what is called a "surge" A surge occurs when liquid in the tanks shifts and pushes the truck forward or backward. This can cause a truck to collide with a stationary vehicle or even be pushed into an intersection. On icy roads, a spill can be especially dangerous because it can cause the truck to roll over. Therefore, it is important to be familiar with how the truck handles, both in good and bad road conditions.

Bulkheads

Tankers with bulkheads are designed to mitigate the effects of wave action and improve sailing stability. By dividing the tank into smaller compartments, the surge is spread over several seconds, minimizing its impact on the ride. You can find out the number of smaller tanks and their respective volumes by inspecting the fittings or checking the owner's manual. It is important to know that one of the smaller tanks may have a slightly different volume, so the timing of the pressure surge will be different for each tank. When filling the tanks, it is important to distribute the weight evenly to avoid putting all the weight on the front or rear of the vehicle.

Baffles

Baffles are internal structures with holes in some tanks designed to reduce the effects of surge during travel by extending the time it takes for the liquid to slosh through the tank. Sloshing baffles look similar to bulkheads, but they do not divide the tank into smaller compartments. Instead, they are placed inside the tank and are designed to help control the surge from front to back. Although they can effectively reduce the effects of surge on handling, bulkheads typically do not have lateral control. It is important that drivers understand the specific structure of the tank they are operating and how the surge baffles or other features can affect driving and safety.

Tanks with Smooth Bore

A smoothbore tank is a type of tank that has no internal surge walls or partitions. This design is used to minimize the ripple effect during transportation. Smooth bore tanks are commonly used for food transportation because they are easier to clean and sanitize compared to tanks with internal structures. Most states have regulations that require food to be transported in smooth bore tanks. Foods that fall under this category include milk, wine, drinking water, fruit juice, and more.

It's important to exercise extra caution when hauling smooth bore tanks to ensure the safety of the driver and the cargo being transported.

Outage

It expands when a liquid is heated. When the cargo heats up, a completely filled tank overflows. There is more space in the upper part of the tank for this expansion. This extra space is called the "spill" Different liquids expand at different rates. Know the extent of the expected spillage.

A Complete Load

Many factors control the maximum quantity of liquid that can be transported in a tank:

1. The liquid weight.

2. Maximum allowed weight limits on public roads.

3. The Gross Combination Weight Ranking (GCWR) of a truck.

4. Tank(s) volume capacity(s).

5. How far the load extends.

6. The load temperature.

Weight limits will "max out" certain bulky loads until the volume of the tank is filled. The tank(s) will be partially filled in these instances. Partially filled tanks compound the surge situation.

Local Legislation

In terms of tankers, some states have extra restrictions. In California, for instance, if you drive a tank vehicle filled with a flammable liquid:

- Speeding brings harsher punishment.
- Service hours are shortened.

Safe Driving

Tanker trucks are far more prone to tipping than a typical commercial vehicle. They have a higher center of gravity and are prone to tipping over sideways and front-to-back. You must also adhere to the following safe driving guidelines:

- Drive effortlessly.
- Start, decelerate, and stop with care.
- Change lanes gradually and with care.
- Brake early.
- Maintain steady pressure on the brakes while braking.
- Do not (when stopping) release your brakes early.
- To drive you forward, expect a surge.
- Increase according to size.
- Know the amount of space it takes to stop.
- If you have to stop quickly, use controlled braking or stag braking.
- Do not steer swiftly. (This might make the truck roll on its side.)
- Slow before curves and slightly accelerate around the curve.
- The posted speed on corners is for cars on dry pavement with strong traction. All trucks can drive at corners slower than the speed indicated. Tankers can drive even slower than other vehicles.
- Double the stopping time on wet roads. Empty vehicles can take longer to stop than vehicles that are loaded.
- Skids
- Do not use unnecessary braking, over accelerate, or over steer. Such stuff can cause a truck to skid.
- Take corrective action if the car begins to skid. A skidding vehicle can jackknife.

If your vehicle starts to jackknife:

- To reestablish traction, release the brakes.

- Reapply the brakes.

Testing Hint

In the written DMV test for tankers, the following unrelated facts might be referenced:

- When entering a tunnel, be prepared to remove sunglasses.
- When exiting a tunnel, expect sudden gusts of wind.

TEST STUDY FOR PASSENGER TRANSPORT FOR THE CDL

How to Prepare for the CDL Passenger Transport Exam

General Information

To legally drive a bus or van that carries passengers, you must obtain a "Passenger Endorsement" as part of your CDL. This is to ensure that drivers have the necessary skills and knowledge to safely operate a large vehicle while caring for passengers. To pass the exam, you will need to master several areas, including vehicle inspection, safety procedures, emergency protocols, operating a vehicle with multiple passengers, proper driver behavior, and adherence to general protocols. However, it is important to note that this study guide only covers the requirements for a basic passenger license and that additional examinations are required to obtain a school bus license.

Who Wants a Passenger Endorsement?

The Confusing Section

A CDL with a passenger endorsement is required to legally drive a vehicle with a certain number of seats, which varies by state. The exact number of seats also varies by state and is usually between 10 and 15. Depending on the state, the driver's seat may or may not be included in the count, and empty seats may or may not be counted. To ensure compliance with your state's laws, it's best to check with your bus company or local DMV for specific requirements. In California, for example, a CDL with a passenger endorsement is required for vehicles designed to carry ten passengers (including the driver) when used for hire or by nonprofit organizations.

Further Limitations

Some insurance companies impose additional restrictions. For example, unless the driver is at least 25 years old, it is common for insurance companies to prohibit drivers from driving a "15-passenger bus" with passengers, even if they have all the required licenses and endorsements.

You must have a passenger endorsement on your CDL to transport passengers, not merely a CLP (Commercial Learner's Permit). You can't drive a bus or van with passengers on board if you just have a CLP, except for:

- The CDL holder(s) (your professor/trainer).
- Fellow driving learners.
- Federal/state test examiner.
- Federal/state auditor(s).
- Federal/state inspector.
- Inspector of automobiles.

Before beginning your morning drive, inspect your car. Here are some things to keep in mind:

- Inspect the seat of the exterior and driver.
- Service brakes.
- Parking brakes.
- Reflectors and lights.
- Horn.
- Wheels, tires, and rims.
- Windshield and wipers.
- Mirrors and/or backing cameras.
- Steering.
- Couplers and air hoses (if pulling a trailer).
- Luggage compartments shut and latched.
- Emergency equipment.
- Equipment hatches closed and latched.
- Emergency exits closed.

Remarks

- Commercial passenger vehicles must be fitted with either an air brake system or a hydraulic system. An air brake endorsement will be required if the vehicle has an air brake system.
- Commercial passenger vehicles should not have steering axle tires recapped or re-grooved.

- On the steering axles of trucks, recapped and/or re-grooved tires are allowed. Recapped and/or re-grooved tires are not used as an industry-standard on any commercial vehicle's steering axles. (You can find recapped and/or re-grooved tires on certain trucks in unique circumstances, but this is unusual.)

The Interior Inspection

Inspection in general

- Seats. (All seats must be tightly connected to the bus.)
- Seat belts. (The driver must always wear a seat belt. If the passenger's seat is fitted with a seat belt, the passenger must wear a seat belt.)
- The windows.
- Emergency exits (operation test).
- Handholds.
- Floor (nothing, but luggage, to go over).
- PA system (if fitted).
- Passenger signaling system(s) (intercom, buzzer, stop-request whistle, etc.)
- It is important to have certain items on board if you operate a commercial motor vehicle. These include a fire extinguisher, emergency equipment such as reflective triangles, and spare fuses if the electrical system is not equipped with circuit breakers. If you carry tools, be sure to store them securely in covered containers so they cannot come loose and pose a safety hazard. It is also important that emergency exits are clearly labeled and that you never drive with the emergency exit open, except for roof hatches. In addition, if there is a red "emergency exit" light attached to the emergency exit, it must be operational at all times or turned on when the headlights are on. These safety measures are important to ensure the safety of the driver, passengers and other road users.

Additional considerations

For better ventilation, you can ride with the escape hatches open. Do not leave the hatches open all the time, especially when the vehicle is parked or unattended.

Note: The bus would be higher with the hatches open, probably taller than the bus's posted clearance height.

Trespassers and vandals will often break into buses or vans and/or destroy them. When you get back, check your car.

Safety

As a CDL driver, it is important that you always wear a seat belt when driving a bus or van. Not only is this for your safety, but it also sets a good example for passengers who are required to wear seat belts if the vehicle is equipped with them. To ensure everyone's safety, make sure luggage is properly stowed and not blocking the aisle or doors. Heavy or sharp objects should be stored securely in covered containers to prevent them from tipping over. Finally, both the driver and passengers must have easy access to emergency exits and be safe from falling or moving objects.

Hazardous Material (Hazmat)

It's crucial to understand the regulations around hazardous materials that can be transported on a bus or van. These regulations can be complex, so it's important to ensure that you know what is and what is not permitted. It's not uncommon for passengers to carry dangerous materials that are unlabeled or unrecognized as prohibited for transportation by bus or truck. Therefore, it's your responsibility as a driver to ensure that no hazardous materials, such as gasoline and car batteries, are carried onboard, including in the passengers' luggage.

All hazmat must be labeled for all three of these:

- The generic name of the chemical.
- A diamond-shaped hazard mark is suggesting the class of Hazmat.
- The content-ID number.

The Hazardous Materials Study Guide covers the laws governing hazardous materials. This study guide covers only the basic regulations for busses and passenger vans.

Your bus company may have additional hazardous materials regulations. Be sure to inquire if you do not know what is allowed.

Note: At the bottom of this section is a map showing the different kinds of hazmat.

Hazmat Summary, Which Can Be Transported by Bus or Van

A bus, if marked ORM-D, can carry handgun ammunition. A bus carries equipment and medications from emergency hospitals. If the shipper cannot transport them by other means, a bus may transport small quantities of other hazardous materials.

Materials That Can Never Be Carried by Bus or Van

Never hold any volume of:

- Poison gas division 2.3.
- Class 6 liquid poison.
- Tear gas.
- Distracting content.
- Explosives (except for small arms ammunition) in the room occupied by people.
- Radioactive content in a room that is occupied by people.

Materials That Can Be Carried by Bus or Van Occasionally

Certain quantities of certain hazmat may be transported; never transport, however:

- More than 100 pounds of Class 6 solid poisons.
- More than 500 pounds of hazmat total allowed.
- Over 100 pounds of any form of hazmat.
- Health oxygen-carrying.

Oxygen is approved for personal use. It must be medically administered and in the possession of the passenger. It must be in a container intended for personal use.

HAZARD CLASS DEFINITIONS		
Class	Class Name	Example
1	Explosives	Ammunition, Dynamite, Fireworks
2	Gases	Propane, Oxygen, Helium
3	Flammable	Gasoline Fuel, Acetone
4	Flammable Solids	Matches, Fuses
5	Oxidizers	Ammonium Nitrate, Hydrogen Peroxide
6	Poisons	Pesticides, Arsenic
7	Radioactive	Uranium, Plutonium
8	Corrosives	Hydrochloric Acid, Battery Acid
9	Miscellaneous Hazardous Materials	Formaldehyde, Asbestos
None	ORM-D (Other Regulated Material-Domestic)	Hair Spray or Charcoal
None	Combustible Liquids	Fuel Oils, Lighter Fluid

Other Questions about Transportation

Wheelchairs

Wheelchairs on busses or vans must also have brakes or be supported in some way when raised or lowered on a rack for elevators. Batteries for wheelchairs (if any) must be leak-proof and securely attached to the wheelchair. Flammable fuel is not permitted.

Note: There are distinct regulations for wheelchairs on school buses.

Animals

It is illegal to transport animals on a public bus or van, except for service dogs. Here are the rules for transporting such dogs:

1. Any person with a disability has the right to be accompanied by a guide dog, signal dog, or support dog specially qualified for the task.

2. Disabled passengers include (but are not limited to):

- A blind or visually impaired passenger.
- A deaf (or hard of hearing) passenger.
- A passenger who needs assistance pulling a wheelchair.
- A passenger who requires notification/protection during a seizure.
- A passenger who must be reminded to take prescription drugs.
- A Post Traumatic Stress Disorder (PTSD) traveler who needs composure during an anxiety attack.

People that are also licensed to have a dog on a bus include:

- A passenger who is licensed to train blind service dogs.
- A passenger who is certified to train dogs for deaf (or hard of hearing) individuals.

1. You may confirm whether an animal is a service animal, but it is illegal to ask for facts and/or proof under Federal law.

2. The concept of "Service Dog" has been extended in recent years (and in some places). Sometimes other species are used. Often state laws do change. If you are uncertain, check with your bus firm or your state DMV.

3. For transporting a service dog, there is never any charge or security deposit necessary. The passenger is, however, liable for any harm done by the dog.

4. The dog should be on a leash and must wear an officially issued service animal "chip" (usually a brightly colored tabard [half coat] with the words "Service Dog").

5. Never try without the owner's express permission to pet, approach, or handle a service dog. The owner's permission would typically be denied.

Remarks

1. It won't be on your written DMV test, but it will be sensitive to the passenger's needs and/or condition. Not all handicaps are easy to see.

2. At present, a hot-button political problem is the inclusion of service animals on buses and other public areas. As a general rule, avoid getting involved in any political issue, including the use of service animals, in a debate/discussion with passengers.

3. Each state has slightly different regulations. The above laws are for California (54.2 of the California Civil Code [CCC]).

RESEARCH GUIDE FOR PASSENGER TRANSPORT FOR THE CDL

Passengers' Treatment

As a bus driver, passenger safety is always your top priority. Before departure, make sure all passengers are seated securely and give standing passengers enough time to brace themselves. It is important that starting, stopping, and turning go smoothly so that the ride is enjoyable for everyone on board. Avoid sudden or abrupt movements that could endanger passenger safety.

The Standee Line

For busses built for standing passengers, there would be a standing line or other signal to let passengers know they cannot stand. A two-inch thick line on the floor is the standing line. Behind this line, every standing passenger must stop.

At Any Stop

Announce it at each stop:

- Location.
- Reasons for stopping.
- Upcoming departure time.
- Number of buses.

Remind passengers to collect their belongings and watch them continue. The best practice is to remind them of a full stop before the bus arrives. Do not allow strangers on the bus unattended. Do not open the bus to passengers until departure time. This serves as a deterrent to vandalism and theft.

Laws, Laws

Most bus companies have laws on smoking, playing music, speaking loudly, etc. To prevent problems later on, clarify the rules before the trip starts.

Mirrors

To observe the passengers when driving, use the interior mirrors. You should need to inform them of the regulations.

In Stops

Passengers should be careful when getting on and off a bus because they can slip. To avoid accidents, passengers should be reminded to watch their step. Each bus company may have specific rules about helping passengers and where to stand when helping passengers. Some busses have steps that can be lowered or stairs that fold in or slide out. It is important that you learn how to operate these features on your bus.

Drunk and/or Disruption Passengers

Each bus company has its own rules for dealing with intoxicated and/or disruptive passengers. Never discharge a passenger in a dangerous location. The best place might be the nearest scheduled stop or a well-lit area where others are.

Evacuating the Bus

If the bus needs to be evacuated, it is necessary for passengers to:

- Offer a short description.
- Told where/how the bus could exit.
- Inform where to go after the bus exit (a mustering place).

Accident Prevention

It is a given that you want to prevent collisions as a bus or van driver. Here are a few things that you have to know:

- Most bus incidents happen at intersections. Even though signals regulate traffic flow, do not presume that other drivers can stop and/or return.

- Know how much space your bus needs. In your mirrors, check for side obstacles. Watch that no things are hitting the back of your mirrors. Check for branches of trees and parked vehicles.

- When you pull from the curb, be mindful that the "nose swing" is contrary to the "tail swing." The rear of your bus swings right (toward the curb) when you steer left (to join traffic).

- Pulling into traffic, make sure there is enough gap for your bus to join the traffic flow. Do not presume that other drivers would stop/slow to let you in.

- A special word on curves: Excessive curve speed is highly hazardous. The bus will be able to turn over with decent traction. The bus could slip off the road with poor traction. If the bus leans toward the outside of a curve, you drive too quickly.

- The "design speed" shown on warning signs is not for buses. "Design speed" is for cars with good traction operating on dry pavement. Reduce speed when in doubt.

Mirrors

When driving a bus, it is important to constantly watch your mirrors. However, be careful not to focus on them for too long or you will be distracted by what is happening in front of the bus. Keep your eyes moving and use proper scanning techniques to improve your situational awareness. There are several types of mirrors on busses, such as wide apartment mirrors (known as "western mirrors") that provide a clear view of the sides and rear of the bus, and convex mirrors (called "target mirrors" or "bullseyes") that provide a wider field of view. Be sure to remember, however, that objects in convex mirrors are closer than they appear.

Stopping needed

Railroad Tracks

Railroad crossings can be very dangerous, and it is not always easy to tell how far away a train is or how fast it is moving. At a grade crossing, there may be multiple tracks and multiple trains to watch out for. In addition, visibility may be limited or obstructed, and not all crossings are equipped with flashing lights or other warning devices. Some crossings rely solely on signs to warn of approaching trains. When approaching a railroad crossing, it is important to use caution and follow proper procedures to ensure your safety and the safety of your passengers.

Avoid Crossing on Any Railroad

Unless you know that it does not require stopping:

- Stop your bus before the railroad crossing, about 15 and 50 feet.
- Listen and look in both directions (open the front door to see or hear if it helps you).

  Note: Sections (or transferred loads) of a damaged railway car can stretch 15 feet over the side of the rail.

- When Stopping Is Not Necessary

Some conditions need no stopping. Slow down and search for other vehicles and trains, but don't stop:

- Railroad tracks running down the center of the road ("street running" railroad).
- At streetcar intersections.
- Where a police officer or flagman guides traffic.
- If the traffic signal displays green.
- At a railway junction designated as "exempt" or "abandoned."
- Additional Information on Railroads
- Ensure that there isn't another train on a parallel track after waiting for a train to pass.
- Never (if you have a manual transmission) change gears when on railroad tracks.
- Never stop on railroad tracks for any car.

About Drawbridge

- Stop on Each Drawbridge

Unless you know that it does not require stopping:

- Stop the bus at least 50 feet before the drawing of the bridge.
- Check (by looking) that the draw is closed entirely.

When Stopping Is Not Necessary

Some conditions need no stopping. Slow down and ensure that it's safe:

- If the bridge has a traffic light that shows green.
- If the bridge has a traffic control officer or attendant who monitors traffic.

Post-Trip (Vehicle Inspection After Trip)

It is important to emphasize the importance of performing pre-trip inspections. Pre-trip inspections are an important part of ensuring the safety of the bus before passengers board. This involves checking the brakes, tires, steering, lights, emergency equipment and other important components of the bus to ensure they are in good working order.

In addition, drivers should be familiar with the bus's emergency procedures and the location of safety equipment. This includes knowing how to exit the bus in an emergency, how to use the fire extinguisher, and how to administer first aid.

By performing pre- and post-trip inspections, drivers can prevent accidents and ensure the safety of their passengers.

Strictly Prohibited

This is a list of stuff that should never be done:

- Never (unless necessary) fuel a bus with passengers on board.
- Never drive a bus with passengers on board in a closed building.
- Never converse while traveling with passengers.
- Never engage yourself in distracting activities while driving.
- Never tow or drive a disabled bus with passengers on board (unless it would be dangerous to let the passengers off). If a disabled bus with passengers on board needs to be towed or moved, simply move the disabled bus to the first safe place where passengers can get off.
- Never use a door interlock instead of setting the brakes for parking.

   Note: When the rear doors of the bus are open, some busses have an interlock that keeps the accelerator pedal in neutral and the transmission in neutral. This is not a substitute for the parking brake being applied and the bus being properly protected.

Stuff That Might Be on Your Written DMV Test

- While checking the interior of the bus, what items are checked?
- What kind of hazmat is transportable by bus?
- What kind of hazmat is not transportable by bus?
- What is a stationary line? How wide is it? How many passengers are required to stand in front of it?
- Where will a disruptive passenger not be released?
- What are some examples of where it is possible to discharge a disruptive passenger?
- How far from the tracks do you stop at a railroad crossing?
- When is it not appropriate for you to stop at a railroad crossing?
- When do you need to pause in front of a drawbridge?
- What are the items shown above on the "Strictly Prohibited" list? (Every one of them.)
- The easiest way to set the parking brakes is to open your bus's rear door?

THE CDL'S DRIVING TEST RESEARCH 1

How to train for the DMV Driving Exam: Basic Control Skills Exam, Vehicle Inspection Test, and Road Test

Until the Driving Test Is Taken

Verify Eligibility

- Obtained the CLP (also known as a Commercial Driver's Instruction Permit [CDIP]).
- Passed the written DMV exams for various endorsements.
- Passed the written DMV test for hazmat and applied for a background check (optional).
- Spent 120–150 hours in the classroom and driving instruction.

  Note: Consult your driving school if you have missed any of these moves. Be sure you are qualified to take the driving test for the DMV.

A Commercial Driver Handbook Review

Get a Handbook for Commercial Drivers. They are available at your local DMV. They are also available online in portable file format (.pdf). You probably already have a copy of the Commercial Driver Handbook if you have gotten this far in the CDL process.

Here is the edition for California. Your state will have a slightly different version of the handbook.

Remarks

- - The section numbers are the section numbers in the California Commercial Driver Handbook in this study guide. The study guide for your state may have different numbers.

- • - The material in this study guide is applicable as much as possible to the driving tests of all states. Each state has numerous laws and different procedures for testing. Use the details in the driver's manual for your state. The first major section of the manual is not very helpful to the learner driver. However, the first large section of this study guide contains many details and references.
- • - The second main part and the third part are outstanding. Therefore, the second and third main parts of this study guide are rather brief and contain Hints.

Information about the Test

There are three aspects of the DMV driving test:

- • Vehicle inspection test (naming all aspects of the test for trucks and air brakes).
- • The basic test of control skills (backed up by the obstacle course).
- • Road test (driving on urban streets and highways).

The testing process will be terminated if you fail any of these tests. (The DMV examiner will not allow you to proceed to the next phase of the testing process if you fail to complete the vehicle inspection.)

If the obstacle course for your DMV is next to the parking lot of the DMV, the driving test would be:

- • Inspection (including a search for air brakes).
- • Basic control.
- • Road test (ending up at the DMV back).

If your DMV's obstacle course was not right next to the DMV parking lot, the driving test would be:

- • Inspection (including a search for air brakes).
- • The first half of the road test (ending at the obstacle course).
- • Basic control.
- • The second half of the road test (ending back at the DMV).

Act and Research Hard

Exact numbers are not available, but industry experts estimate that 80 to 90 percent of learner drivers pass the DMV driving test on the first try. That means ten to 20 percent fail the test on the first try.

This is not unique to high school. The DMV examiner will fail you if you are unprepared.

General consulting

Hey, Stay Calm

Remain calm throughout the exam. This exam is designed so that almost anyone who has studied and practiced can pass it. You should not have too much difficulty once you have read it.

The examiner will not deceive you. The examiner will not ask you to do anything illegal or dangerous. The examiner wants you to pass.

Be Ready and Rested

Being able to relax before the test:

- Get a full evening's sleep.
- Arrive with plenty of time at the testing site.
- Before beginning, take several long, soothing breaths.

Practice Before

You should be able to do the following before you take the DMV driving test:

- Inspect the vehicle (under the hood, outside the vehicle, and in the cab).
- Conduct an air brake test.
- Drive the truck back through the obstacle course.
- The truck runs safely on city streets and highways.
- Smoothly Change.

Understand the Local Process

Below I explain the process by which I passed the exam. My teachers were familiar with the local admissions office. I was trained to take the exam the way the examiners at the local licensing board wanted me to. You are instructed by your teachers to take the test the way the local licensing board examiners want you to take it. But the basic values remain the same.

Wisely Use Planning Time

It's important to make the most of your time in driver's ed by actively observing your fellow students, practicing your skills on the practice range, and studying for tests like the vehicle inspection test. This will help you prepare for the DMV driving test and ensure that you are well-equipped to handle various scenarios on the road. Instead of wasting time talking to classmates, focus on learning and improving your skills. Remember that good preparation is the key to passing the driving test and becoming a safe and responsible driver.

Anticipate All Potential Costs and Scenarios

A reputable truck driving school will usually offer you two opportunities to take the driving test as part of your tuition, and will provide you with one of their trucks for a third attempt if needed. The cost of renting the truck is $50-$100, and the school will also help schedule medical exams, DMV licensing exams, and scheduling the driving test. However, if you enroll in a major trucking company's program that includes training and work, you are usually only allowed two attempts at the driving test. If you fail three times, you will be dropped from the program and still have to pay for training. If you fail the driving test three times, you will have to start the process over by applying for a CLP and retaking the written tests.

Consider These Points, Too

- The examiners are trying to see if you can handle the equipment and are competent.
- You must speak English throughout the exam. You will be warned up to two times if you speak a language other than English or do not understand the examiner's instructions. On the third violation, you will automatically be considered to have failed the exam.
- To help you with the exam, you cannot use notes.

THE CDL'S DRIVING TEST RESEARCH 2

The Inspection Exam for Vehicles

The inspection test will be the first test you take. Here you will have to identify the different parts of the truck and clarify what to look for during an inspection.

Underlying Process

For detailed information on inspecting each part of the truck, see the diagrams and descriptions in the CDL manual ("SECTION 11: VEHICLE INSPECTION TEST"). The diagrams and explanations do not provide valuable information on how to inspect the entire truck or pass this inspection.

There are three parts of the truck that you can inspect:

- Under the hood.
- The outside of the truck.
- The inside of the cab (including testing for air brakes).

Still search the same way. Start in the same corner and work in the same direction around the truck. One sure way to get confused and/or miss something is to "take turns" or "skip"

You will not be tested during this exam. The examiner needs to make sure you know how to inspect items. For example, point to the dipstick and say, "Check the oil level" You do not take the dipstick out and check the oil level.

Remarks

1. Follow the inspector's instructions when the inspector asks you to check the oil level.

2. If the inspection check must be stopped, explain why you are stopping: "I am checking to see if the parking brake is on." "I am getting my gloves out of my pocket."

71

Warning: Gloves to wear. Don't burn the hot engine components yourself.

The Three Areas of Inspection

Underneath the Hood

Start at the front and work your way to the windshield (front to back and top to bottom). Check systematically in the same way each time:

- Grill.
- Radiator mounts.
- Radiator.
- Fan and fan blades.
- Belt.
- Fan clutch.
- Compressor.

You should be able to rattle off the entire list of parts and what you are looking for:

"Grill: no injuries, no clogs. Radiator: no damage, no clogs, no leaks, no rust marks. Brackets for radiator: sturdy, no damage, no bolts missing, nothing bent. Fan and fan blades: firmly installed, no injuries, no blades missing, no cracks. Fan clutch: the fan rotates by hand, not free. Belt: no missing belts, no cracks, three-quarter belt flexes when pressed with a finger. Compressor: firmly installed, no injuries, no missing screws, stable pulley, etc."

Point and/or touch as you name each part.

> Note: The inspection will be on the driver's side (where most sections are), but they will be prepared to clear the passenger's side.

> Warning: Switching off the engine before going under the hood for inspection.

The Truck's Exterior

Start at the driver (where the previous inspection ends) and work your way counterclockwise around the track. Name the parts as you go.

The inspector may not want you to inspect the other side of the truck after you have inspected one side and the rear of the truck. The examiner may direct you back to the front of the vehicle. You may be interrupted by the interviewer with questions. Answer the questions and then ask if you should continue or not.

Interior of the Cab

Make sure you set the parking brake - chair change. Name the various controls. Especially the brakes, lights, and wipers. Change the mirror at this point. (Do not be afraid to ask the examiner to help you change the passenger side mirror)

A brake test would need to be performed at this point. The brake test is listed in our brake test study guide.

Test-Taking Advice

Describe what you are doing during the investigation and what you are looking for. Point to things as you explain them. (Pointing helps you remember.) Touch the items as you explain them. (Touching helps you remember.) It is easier to touch something than to point.

In general, you can look for the following when inspecting equipment:

- Missing bolts.
- Obstructions.
- Damage.
- Foreign objects.
- Streaks of rust or shiny spots on metal surfaces (which may mean loose bolts).
- On-ground puddles (leaks).
- Bent parts.
- Splashes of liquids.
- Puddles on the ground (leaks).
- Wires hanging loose.
- Sounds of leaking air.
- Damage to the truck.
- Frayed wire/hoses.

Note: For examiners, duct tape is a "red flag."

The Skills Test for Basic Controls

"Basic Controls", without crossing a boundary or driving over a traffic cone, effectively assists the truck in crossing an obstacle course.

Underlying Process

The summary in the CDL Handbook for this section is excellent ("SECTION 12: BASIC CONTROL SKILLS TEST"). The assessment process ("12.1—Scoring") and the measures ("12.2—Exercises") are defined clearly.

Test-Taking Advice

Similar to the nearby DMV test course, the nearby driving school will also set up the obstacle course.

A Puzzle

The backing is like a puzzle or a complicated shot at billiards - imagine what you will do. Decide where you want your trailer to go from the back. Decide when you want the steering wheel to go into reverse. Stop and think again if the trailer is going the wrong way. Three to five seconds can make all the difference.

Get a free pull-up on every exercise except straight-line backing. (You do not receive free pull-ups during straight-line backing.) Any pull-up after the first free pull-up counts as a failure.

Stopping does not count as a pull-up without a change of direction. Stop and look out the window (and/or in the mirrors) if you are distracted or want to waste a few seconds staring at the alternate scenario. This will not count against you as long as you continue in the same direction (do not change direction).

The "Looks"

Put the truck in neutral and set the parking brake. You may exit and "look" Exit the truck safely (with three points of contact). You may "look" twice (except when backing in a straight line, where you may "look" once).

It counts as a "look" if you open the door or rise from a seated position.

The Steering First

You steer the first axle as you go forward, so all the other axles follow. If you drive backwards, the same thing happens. The most critical factor is the first axle (which is the last axle on the trailer if you are going backwards). Get the rear axle in place, then the tractor drive axles, then the tractor steering axles. If the rear axles of the trailer move to the wrong position, focus again on this axle, etc.

The Test of the Road

This test requires driving in several road conditions. A combination of street driving, highway driving, turns to navigate, etc., will be available.

Underlying Process

This section of the CDL manual ("SECTION 13: ROAD TEST") is excellent.

The examiner will tell you where to drive. You will not be told by the examiner to do anything illegal or dangerous. You will be given ample time to perform the required maneuvers.

You will be driven to a side road if there are no such traffic conditions on the practice route, and the examiner will ask you to recreate the scenario. (For example, there are no railroad tracks in your town.)

Test-Taking Suggestions

- Before you leave, make sure the mirrors are fully adjusted. (Do not be afraid to ask the inspector to help you change the passenger side mirror) When you drive off, stop and change the mirrors if they are not correct. You will probably get the point deducted, but it's better than crashing. (Inform the inspector why you want to stop)
- Keep the truck in gear (except when shifting). If your truck is longer than a truck, you automatically lose.
- Constantly scan the windows, check the mirrors, test the gages, etc.
- Check the mirrors more frequently while rotating.
- Wear a seat belt.
- Drive cautiously.

Summary

Get a professional driver's manual from your state. Read only that. The "Basic Control Skills Test" and "Road Test" parts are really good. The "Vehicle Inspection Test" part is not very descriptive. Ask your driving instructor for information on how the "Vehicle Inspection Test" is administered by your local DMV.

Review the Material in the Handbook

Be attentive in class. Observe what your fellow students are doing. But do not waste time. Standing around chatting with your fellow students is very easy, but if you do too much of it, you will not be prepared for your driving test.

GUIDE TO GENERAL KNOWLEDGE TEST ANALYSIS FOR THE CDL

How to Prepare for the Test of CDL General Knowledge

General Information

In order to perform their jobs with the utmost safety and success, it is critical for commercial driver's license holders to know and follow the relevant guidelines. This study guide is intended to provide a brief overview of these guidelines to help drivers perform their jobs to the best of their ability. It is important that you read the special medical considerations at the end of this guide before beginning any driving instructions or testing procedures.

Inspection of Automobiles

Every time you check your car, taking the same steps will help minimize the chances of missing an important safety hazard or defect.

The Pre-Trip Inspection Seven Phases Process

Make sure always to follow the seven-step pre-trip inspection process before you embark on any trip. Here are the phases that this approach includes:

Phase 1: Description of Vehicles

1. Notice the vehicle's general state.

2. Look under the vehicle for leaks or puddles of fluid.

3. To see if there were any concerns and if they have been corrected, review the last written Vehicle Inspection Report (VIR).

Phase 2: Engine Compartment Search

1. Make sure the wheels are tight or that the parking brakes are applied.

2. Check that all engine fluids are at optimum level.

3. Look for loose cables, hoses, and belts.

4. Check for broken or worn insulation on cables.

5. Close the hood of an engine.

Warning: Never inspect the motor compartment inside when the engine is running.

Phase 3: Start and Inspect the Engine Inside the Cab

1. Set the brakes for parking. Place the gear shift (or "park" if automatic) in neutral.

2. Get the engine started. Please search for odd noises coming from the engine.

3. Look at the gauges to make sure that each fits within a standard range. (The alarm lights and buzzers will be extinguished in a few seconds.)

4. Check to see if any of the levers feel loose or sticky.

5. Double-check whether the truck is fitted with appropriate protective equipment, such as a fire extinguisher and reflective triangles.

6. Windshield check. Switch mirrors.

Note: The oil pressure gauge should show five psi (or more) within three to five seconds when starting an engine. Shut the engine off if the oil pressure indicates no rise after five seconds. Within 30 seconds, the oil pressure gauge will stable above 50 psi.

Phase 4: Engine Shutdown and Lights Check

1. Set the parking brakes, switch the engine off, and turn on the four-way flashers and headlights.

2. When you head towards the front of the car, take the key with you.

3. Go back into the cab of the car and press the dimmer switch if you are sure that all lights are operational.

4. Go back to the front of the vehicle to guarantee that the high beams work.

Phase 5: Inspect Walking

1. Turn on your indicators for the right turn. Start walking around the car.

2. Ensure that all tires are in good shape and that the lamps are free of dirt and running.

3. The suspension and brakes should work.

4. There should be no leaks in the fuel tank, exhaust system, and transmission.

5. Ensure that the cargo is secured properly and that the signs/placards needed are displayed correctly.

6. Make sure there are latched, secured, and sealed rear doors.

7. Verify that the license plate is in place and protected.

8. It is essential to shut and latch all hatches and toolboxes. (A simple sign that something is loose, scratching, or moving is shiny patches of metal or streaks of rust.)

Phase 6: Signal Lights Search

1. Turn off all previously checked lights and turn on the signs for stoplights and left turns.

2. To make sure that the lights flash the correct color, go outside the vehicle (if required).

3. Amber or white should be the signals facing the front of the car.

4. Amber, red, or yellow should be the signals facing the rear of the vehicle.

5. The rear support lights (if equipped) should be white.

6. Switch off all of the unwanted lights for driving.

7. Finish your preparation for your journey.

8. Check that you have all the paperwork available.

9. In the car, secure any loose objects. Only fasten the seatbelt.

Phase 7: Launch the Hydraulic Leak Engine Test and Check

1. Get the engine started.

2. Hydraulic brakes (if equipped) should be checked by pressing the brake pedal three times, then holding the pedal for five seconds; the pedal should not move.

3. Push the car forward and the parking brake will be applied. Release it and observe if the parking brake works. Drive about five miles per hour and press hard on the brake pedal. You have a

problem with the brake if you notice a pulling to the side or an unusual feeling on the pedal. Before you begin your ride, troubleshoot these problems.

Note (between phase 6 and 7): It is not part of any DMV exam, but gathering anything you need during your driving shift (placing everything within easy reach) before starting the engine and setting off is usually considered healthy, safe practice:

- Glasses.
- Trip plan.
- Sunglasses.
- Pens/pencils.
- Logbook.
- Maps.
- Music.
- Beverages and snacks.

During the Trip Inspection

Inspect your truck within the first 50 miles and every 150 miles or every three hours (whichever comes first) during your trip. Make sure your cargo and truck equipment is still safe, your tires are still in good condition, and your brakes are not overheating. While driving, periodically check the operating condition of the vehicle (instruments, gages, air pressure, mirrors, check tires by looking in mirrors, etc.). Fill out a Vehicle Inspection Report (VIR) after your ride, noting anything that needs to be addressed to maintain or protect the vehicle.

Other Safeguards for Protection

Keeping yourself and other drivers as safe as possible when driving is crucial. Here are some additional important methods.

Safely Back Up the Trailer

To maximize visibility, avoid backing up your trailer whenever possible. If you must reverse, drive on the driver's side (left). Unlike a straight vehicle, when backing up with a trailer, you must turn the steering wheel in the opposite direction you want to go. Use your mirrors and drive slowly. Correct any drifting by turning the steering wheel in the direction in which you want to drive.

GOAL in Case of Doubt

To investigate what is behind the trailer or out of sight, even seasoned drivers stop what they are doing, open the door, and climb out of the truck.

Caution as You Drive

Every action you take requires extra time and thought due to the length of commercial semi-trucks. Try to look ahead 12-15 seconds while driving to ensure you have enough time to react to changes in topography, traffic, and difficult road conditions. Use your mirrors, but do not look into them for too long. What comes next should always be your top priority.

Communicating

Let other drivers know what you plan to do by using your turn signals. Turn them on in advance and leave them on until you have turned. If you see a hazard, such as a rock in the road, step lightly on the brake pedal to make your brake lights come on. This will alert drivers behind you to potential hazards, especially since visibility is limited by the height of your truck. If you ever have to stop at the side of the road, set up your reflective triangles within ten minutes of stopping.

Managing Space

Since your vehicle is significantly larger than most other vehicles on the road, you need to allow more space in front of you to come to a stop. A good rule of thumb is that at speeds below 40 miles per hour, you should allow one second of stopping distance for every ten feet of vehicle length. If you are traveling faster than 40 miles per hour, allow an additional second. For example, a truck 50 feet long traveling 60 miles per hour would need six seconds to stop (five seconds for the length of the vehicle plus one second for exceeding 40 miles per hour). Please note that road conditions, such as slippery roads or inclines, can affect your stopping distance, so adjust your speed accordingly.

Hint: You can see these numbers on your written CDL exam.

Safely Make Turns

When turning left, wait until you reach the intersection before turning. In situations where there are multiple turn lanes, it is advisable to take the outside right lane instead of the inside left lane. The reason for this is that you need to veer to the right to turn, and if you turn in the left lane, you could collide with the car next to you. If you need to turn right and go wide, it's best to keep the rear of your vehicle close to the curb to prevent other drivers from trying to pass you on the right.

Dealing With Difficult Road Conditions

To increase your chances of a successful trip, it is important to know how to deal with different types of bad weather or difficult terrain. Even on hot, sunny days, tar can make the roads slippery. Be careful, turn on your low beams, and use your brakes if you have to drive in fog. When driving in mountainous areas, shift to a lower gear before going down a hill, and drive slowly enough that you do not have to use your brakes too often. Frequent application of the brakes can cause them to overheat and fail. If you are driving through a large puddle and your brakes get muddy, shift to a low gear and press lightly on the brakes. After leaving the puddle, continue to apply light pressure to the brakes to dry and warm them up.

Relevant Meanings

Ratings on Weight

1. The actual weight of a vehicle (straight truck), including its load, is Gross Vehicle Weight (GVW).

2. The maximum weight rating (straight truck) of the manufacturer, including its load, is Gross Vehicle Weight Rating (GVWR).

3. Gross Combination Weight (GCW) is the same as GVW, but for a combination vehicle (with a trailer).

4. Except for a hybrid vehicle (with a trailer), the Gross Combination Weight Classification (GCWR) is the same as the GVWR. (Pounds 80,000 generally.)

Service Hours

HOS stands for Hours of Service. HOS regulations limit how many hours a driver may work and/or drive in a single shift. They also regulate the minimum number of rest periods between work shifts that a driver must be granted.

Facts Bonus

1. Be prepared when entering a tunnel to remove sunglasses.

2. When leaving a tunnel, expect unexpected gusts of wind.

Medical Requirements

To drive a commercial vehicle, you must obtain an Official Medical Examination Report form (MER), formerly known as a "medical card" You can obtain this form only if you undergo a medical examination conducted by a certified medical examiner, usually a physician. It is important to know that not all physicians are authorized to issue MERs, as they must follow a specific certification process.

The examiner will mainly review your:

1. Vision (with glasses or without).

2. Hearing.

3. Fat in the urine (diabetes).

Diabetes

You can also get medical approval if you have type 2 diabetes and do not use insulin. You could get a one-year MER (instead of the usual two years MER) with type 2 diabetes.

Seizures

You do not qualify for an MER if you have seizures.

An exception

Individuals with certain medical conditions, such as diabetes, hearing impairments, seizures, or visual impairments, may be exempt from the requirement to submit a medical examination report (MER). Instead, they receive a "medical exemption" To obtain a medical exemption, you can submit an application to the Federal Motor Carrier Safety Administration (FMCSA), which takes up to six months to make a decision. It's important to know that the exemption only applies to interstate travel. Some states may also grant waivers for medications, but these are only valid for intrastate travel (within the state).

Plan Ahead

If you think that you have no chance to apply for a MER before wasting time, effort and money on driving school, it is better to try to get it.

When looking for an examiner, the driving school will assist you and educate you about MERs and waivers.

SCHOOL BUS ENDORSEMENT

To drive a yellow school bus with 16 or more seats, including the driver, CDL holders must first pass the sensitivity test to obtain a school bus permit. If the bus has air brakes, they must also pass the air brake test. In addition, they must pass the skill and driving tests for the class of license applied for. A school bus license is required if you transport primary, preschool, or secondary students to and from school or school-sponsored activities.

CDL school bus drivers who do not have the (S) School Bus Endorsement are not legally allowed to drive a yellow school bus.

The Criteria

A driver has to:

- Be 21 years old or older.
- Possess a valid driver's license issued by the Secretary of State and properly classified.
- When required, possess a current medical card.
- Successfully pass a written school bus endorsement test conducted by the Secretary of State.
- Pass a driving test successfully, if necessary, in a representative license class vehicle for passenger and school bus endorsements.
- Not being repeatedly involved as drivers in collisions involving motor vehicles or often convicted of traffic offenses, showing contempt for traffic laws.

Safety Information

Inspection of Pre-Trip

It is the responsibility of the driver to conduct a daily inspection of the mechanical and safety equipment of the school bus before it is placed in service. Under administrative law, no one other than the driver may perform the inspection prior to the start of the trip. Upon completion of the inspection, the driver must complete a School Bus Driver Pre-Operation Inspection Form documenting any deficiencies found on the bus.

Limits on Speeds

When driving a school bus, remember that the maximum speed is generally the same as that of a car. However, because of the size and weight of a school bus, it requires a longer stopping distance than a normal passenger vehicle. This means that you should watch your speed and slow down in front of potential hazards such as intersections, sharp turns, or heavy traffic. It's also important to adjust your driving to the time of day, weather conditions, and road conditions. In bad weather, such as rain or snow, you should reduce your speed even further to allow more time to stop. Also, always be aware of the actions of other drivers around you and be prepared to react accordingly.

Entering the Expressway or Leaving It

Do it as simply and as safely as possible when entering or leaving an expressway. Never bring your car to a stop immediately before entering an expressway unless necessary. Enter and merge into moving traffic as safely as possible.

Take Them Safely

- When you stop to load and unload students, you can better control traffic by observing the safety measures on the school bus.
- At a minimum, the yellow lights on the eight-lamp flashing system must be triggered when approaching a stop:
- One hundred feet outside the city limits.
- Two hundred feet outside the city limits.
- When loading or unloading, come to a complete stop, place the transmission in the "neutral park" position, and apply the parking brake.
- No child shall cross a street with four or more travel lanes where at least one or more travel lanes are in the opposite direction. The student's residence and/or school (attendance center) must be on the right side of the highway in order to locate the school bus stop.
- The driver may only let students off the school bus at designated stops. This procedure is designed to provide maximum safety for you and your passengers, but limiting additional stops

also saves fuel. Do not change routes or pick-ups without the required permission from the school board.

- The service door must be closed at all times while the vehicle is in motion.
- The emergency door must be open but firmly locked while the school bus is in operation (if equipped with a lock).
- Do not exceed the provider's capacity for a bus.
- Students may not be asked to leave the bus on the street for discipline violations, nor may they be asked to sit anywhere other than in a seat.
- If students are in the vicinity, the driver may return the bus to school only if a responsible person is present to direct the bus driver.
- The bus may be driven onto school grounds to dismiss students or they should be dismissed so that they do not have to cross a path. The driver must direct students to walk at least three feet in front of the bus on the side of the road at all dismissal points where students must cross a roadway and remain there until the bus driver signals them to cross.
- The driver shall not permit a student to disembark from the bus at a location other than the student's designated exit point unless written permission is granted by the appropriate school official.
- The driver must stop between 15 and 50 feet before the first rail of the grade crossing. Place the transmission in the "neutral park" position and apply the parking brake when stopping. When a train is approaching, the driver must open the service door and driver's window, listen and look both ways. If the driver determines that no train is approaching, he or she must close the door and cross the grade crossing completely in low gear.
- Before setting the bus in motion, the driver's seat belt must always be properly fastened.
- The driver and/or controller must walk through the bus after parking it for the day to ensure that no child is left behind.

GENERAL KNOWLEDGE
PRACTICE TEST

Instructor: _____   Date: _____

Name: _____

Directions: The General Knowledge Practice Test has 100 questions. Before you can take the other CDL tests, you must pass a test similar to this one.

For each question, there is only one correct answer. Answer all your questions and CIRCLE your replies.

1. There should be at least one tie-down for each cargo foot to prevent a load from moving.

   A. 15.

   B. Ten.

   C. 20.

2. At 35 mph, you're driving a 40-foot truck. The road is dry, and there is decent visibility. What is the minimum amount of safe space that you can hold in front of your vehicle?

   A. Two seconds.

   B. Four seconds.

   C. Six seconds.

3. You are traveling down a long, steep hill. Your brakes get so hot that they fail. What should you do?

   A. Downshift.

   B. Look escape route or for an escape ramp.

   C. Pump the brake pedal.

4. The gravity core of a load:

   A. It should be held as high as you can.

   B. If it is heavy, it can make a vehicle more likely to tip over on curves.

   C. It is only a concern when the vehicle is overloaded.

5. Which of these statements about drinking alcohol is true?

   A. A few beers have the same effect on driving as a few shots of whiskey or a few glasses of wine.

   B. Coffee and fresh air will help a drinker sober up.

   C. Not everyone who drinks is affected by alcohol.

6. What is the proper way to hold a steering wheel?

   A. With both hands close together, near the top of the wheel.

   B. With both hands close together, near the bottom of the wheel.

   C. With your hand's place on opposite sides of the wheel.

7. You do not have a Hazardous Materials Endorsement on your Commercial Driver's License. You can drive a vehicle hauling hazardous materials when:

   A. The vehicle doesn't require placards.

   B. The shipment won't cross state lines.

   C. A person who has the Hazardous Materials Endorsement rides with you.

8. What is known as countersteering?

   A. Steering in the opposite direction from what other drivers expect you to.

   B. Turning the wheel back in the other direction after steering to avoid a traffic emergency.

   C. Using the steering axle brakes to prevent oversteering.

9. Retarders:

   A. Reduce brake wear.

   B. Are needed only when hazardous materials are being hauled.

C. Allow you to disconnect the steering axle brakes.

10. When driving, ice builds up on the wipers, and they no longer clean the windshield. You should do:

    A. Keep driving and turn your defroster on.

    B. Stop safely and fix the problem.

    C. Keep driving and spray the windshield with washer fluid.

11. When you drive a new truck with a manual transmission, what gear will you probably have to use to take a long, steep downhill grade?

    A. A lower gear than you would use to climb the hill.

    B. The same gear you would use to climb the hill.

    C. A higher gear than you would use to climb the hill.

12. Which of these statements about driving in areas with strong winds is true?

    A. Winds are a big problem when a truck comes out of a tunnel.

    B. You should drive alongside other vehicles to help break up the wind.

    C. The lighter your vehicle, the less trouble you will have with the wind.

13. Cargo inspections:

    A. Should be performed after every break you take while driving.

    B. Are most often not the responsibility of the driver.

    C. Are needed only if hazardous materials are being hauled.

14. To help you stay alert while driving, you should:

    A. Take cold medicine if you have a cold.

    B. Schedule trips for hours you are normally asleep.

    C. Take short breaks before you get drowsy.

15. One of the statements about double-clutching and shifting is true:

    A. Only with a heavy load can double-clutching be used.

    B. Double clutching when the road is slippery should not be used.

    C. The tachometer can be used to tell when to move.

16. One of the statements about cargo loading is true:

    A. State laws dictate limitations on legal weight.

    B. For all driving conditions, the maximum legal weight permitted by a state can be considered safe.

C. The driver is not responsible for overloading if the shipper loads the freight.

17. Which of these statements about marking a stopped vehicle is true?

    A. Shift the rear reflective triangle back down the road to provide sufficient warning if a hill or curve stops drivers behind you from seeing the vehicle within 500 feet.

    B. If the car is stopped for 30 minutes or more, you do not need to put out reflective triangles.

    C. To warn other drivers, the vehicle's taillights should be kept on.

18. Every time you leave your vehicle, you should:

    A. Switch as far to the left of the steering wheel as you can.

    B. With the brake applied.

    C. Leave it in gear (if it has a manual transmission).

19. A vehicle is loaded with very little weight on the drive axle. What may happen?

    A. Poor traction.

    B. Better handling.

    C. Damage to drive axle tires.

20. Which of these best describes how you should use the brake pedal on a steep downhill grade?

    A. Light, constant pressure.

    B. Strong repeated pressure, then release.

    C. When the vehicle goes downhill, with stronger friction.

21. Which of these statements about speed management is true?

    A. Empty trucks often stop at a distance shorter than fully loaded trucks.

    B. It will take twice the distance to stop when you double your speed (go twice as fast).

    C. You can choose a pace that helps you to stop within the distance you can see ahead of you.

22. Which of these statements about using turn signals is true?

    A. When changing lanes on a four-lane highway in traffic, you do not need to use your turn signal.

    B. You can signal early on when turning.

    C. When it is pulled off at the side of the lane, you can use your turn signal to identify your car.

23. An en route inspection should include checking for:

    A. Tire overheating and brake overheating.

    B. Cargo securement.

C. Both of the above.

24. When are you checking your tires for a pre-trip inspection, which of these statements is true?

    A. It is not appropriate to use tires of mismatched sizes on the same vehicle.

    B. For the front tires, a tread depth of 2/32 inches is healthy.

    C. Radial and bias-ply tires on the same vehicle can be used together.

25. You are driving a four-lane, undivided road in the right lane. You're going up a hill, and you find a car stopped in front of you in your path. You have no place to pause. To the rear, the hill blocks your vision. There's a clear side. Which of these is the best step to take?

    A. Steer to the right.

    B. Steer into the left lane.

    C. Use hard braking and brace for collision.

26. If your vehicle catches fire while you are driving, you should:

    A. Park in an open area.

    B. Increase your speed to put out the flames.

    C. Park where a building or trees shelter your vehicle from the wind.

27. Which of the following is a good thing to do when driving at night?

    A. Look just momentarily directly at the oncoming headlights.

    B. Keep your velocity slow enough to stop within the range of your headlights.

    C. Keep the lights of your instrument short.

28. While driving, how far ahead of the truck should a driver look?

    A. One–two seconds.

    B. Five–eight seconds.

    C. 12–15 seconds.

29. You see a marking on a vehicle ahead of you (the marking is a red triangle with an orange center). What does the marking mean?

    A. It may be a slow-moving vehicle.

    B. It is a law enforcement vehicle.

    C. The vehicle is hauling hazardous materials.

30. How can you test hydraulic brakes for leaks?

    A. Push down the pedal firmly for five seconds and see if it moves.

    B. Measure the free play in the pedal with a ruler.

C. Move the vehicle slowly and see if it stops when you put on the brakes.

31. Refer to the figure below for this question. You drive a long vehicle that makes wide turns. You want to make a left turn from Elm Street onto Oak Street. There are two lanes on Elm Street that turn left (marked "A" and "B"). Oak Street is a four-lane street in either direction with two lanes. Should You:

    A. Use left turn lane "A."

    B. Use left turn lane "B."

    C. Begin in the left-turn lane "A" and swing into left lane "B" just before entering the intersection.

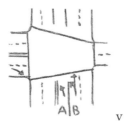

Left turn diagram (for use with question 31)

32. Cargo covers:

    A. In certain states, it could be a safety necessity.

    B. Secure individuals from spilled cargo.

    C. Both of the above.

33. Where or when should you test the stopping action of your service brakes?

    A. When the vehicle is not moving, in a parking lot.

    B. At a special Brake Testing Center only.

    C. When the truck is moving at five mph.

34. Which of the following statements about backing a heavy vehicle is true?

    A. Whenever you may, you can stop backing.

    B. Helpers should be out of sight of the driver and communicate with the driver using only voice (spoken) signals.

    C. It is better to go back to the truck's right side than to the driver's side.

35. Which of the following is not part of the pre-trip inspection of the engine compartment?

    A. Valve clearance.

B. Worn electrical wiring insulation.

C. Condition of hoses.

36. Which of the following statements about managing space is true?

    A. Many accidents are caused by drivers holding too much room in front of their vehicles.

    B. Smaller vehicles need more room than larger ones to stop.

    C. You need a lot of space to stop when the road is slippery.

37. You must park on the side of a level, straight, two-lane road. Where should you place the reflective triangles?

    A. One is ten feet from the rear of the vehicle, one is 100 feet from the rear, and one is 200 feet from the rear.

    B. One is ten feet from the rear of the vehicle, one is 100 feet from the rear of the vehicle, and one is 100 feet from the front of the vehicle.

    C. One to the back of the vehicle about 50 feet, one to the back about 100 feet, and one to the front of the vehicle about 100 feet.

38. High beams should be:

    A. Used when it is safe to do so and legal.

    B. Dimmed at the moment that you get to another vehicle within 100 feet.

    C. Turned on when their lights are not dimmed by an oncoming car.

39. Which of the following statements about drugs is true?

    A. Any prescription medicine can be used by a driver when driving.

    B. Drug use can lead to crashes and/or arrests.

    C. The above are both real.

40. You want to turn right from one two-lane, two-way street to another. Your vehicle is so long that to make the turn, you must swing wide. Which of these figures indicates how long it is appropriate to make the turn?

    A. Figure A.

    B. Figure B.

    C. Figure C.

93

FIGURE A   FIGURE B   FIGURE C

RIGHT TURN SITUATIONS

41. Which of these is the most important thing to remember about emergency braking?

    A. During emergency braking, the steering axle brakes' disconnection can help hold the vehicle in a straight line.

    B. You cannot steer the vehicle if the wheels are skidding.

    C. Never do it without first downshifting.

42. Your truck is in a traffic emergency, and if you do not take action, it may collide with another car. At such a time, which of these is a good rule to remember?

    A. You will almost always turn around and miss an obstacle quicker than you can pause.

    B. In a traffic emergency, stopping is always the best step.

    C. It is often more dangerous to abandon the road than to hit another car.

43. You start your car from the stop. As you add power to the drive wheels, they start to rotate. Should you:

    A. Take the accelerator off your foot.

    B. Push harder the accelerator.

    C. Try the smaller gear.

44. The road on which you drive becomes very slippery due to the glare of ice. Which of these, in such a situation, is a good thing to do?

    A. As soon as you can comfortably do so, stop driving.

    B. Downshift to pause.

    C. To keep the linings dry, apply the brakes sometimes.

45. What do you do when hydroplanes are in your vehicle?

    A. Slightly Accelerate.

    B. Difficult counter steering.

    C. Accelerator release.

94

46. To fix a drive-wheel braking skid, you should:

    A. Stop braking, turn, and counter-steer easily.

    B. Increase braking.

    C. Increase the braking, rapidly turn, and counter steer.

47. Which of these claims is accurate for downshifting?

    A. You can do so before you reach the curve when you downshift for a curve.

    B. You can do so before you hit the curve as you downshift toward a slope.

    C. When double-clutching, when the clutch is released and the shift lever is neutral, you can let the RPMs decrease.

48. Which one of these tires and hot-weather driving claims is true?

    A. A tire's air pressure decreases as the tire's temperature increases.

    B. You should drive on it to cool off when a tire is too hot to touch.

    C. When driving in very hot weather, you can check your tires every two hours or every 100 miles.

49. What fires can you put out with the use of water?

    A. Fires with fuel.

    B. Electric fireplaces.

    C. Fires with tires.

50. Stab braking:

    A. Never to be used.

    B. It just requires releasing the brakes after the wheels have locked up.

    C. Without locking the wheels, the brake pedal requires constant pressure.

51. It takes the body about _____ hours to get rid of four drinks of alcohol.

    A. Six.

    B. Two.

    C. Four.

52. Cargo that can shift should have at least _____ tie-down(s).

    A. One.

    B. Two.

    C. Three.

53. When the roads are slippery, you should:

A. Drive alongside other vehicles.

B. Make turns as gently as possible.

C. Stop and test the traction while going up hills.

54. When a straight vehicle goes into a front-wheel skid (no trailer or articulation), you should:

    A. Slide yourself sideways and spin out.

    B. Go straight ahead, even though you turn the steering wheel.

    C. Go straight ahead, but if you turn the steering wheel, you can turn.

55. Which of these claims is accurate about the brakes?

    A. When they get really heavy, the brakes have more stopping power.

    B. When the car is going very fast, brake drums cool very quickly.

    C. The heavier a car is, the faster it drives, and the more heat the brakes need to handle to stop it.

56. When driving through work zones, you should:

    A. Turn your flashers on and slowly drive.

    B. To warn drivers behind you, use your brake lights.

    C. Do all the above.

57. You are driving a truck at 55 mph on dry pavement. How much total stopping distance are you going to need to bring it to a stop?

    A. Twice the vehicle's length.

    B. Half of a football field's length.

    C. The length of the field of football.

58. You are driving a big truck. You must exit a highway using an off-ramp that curves downhill. Should you:

    A. Before the curve, slow down to a safe pace.

    B. For the off-ramp, slow to the posted speed limit.

    C. Before downshifting, wait until you're in the curve.

59. When crossing or approaching traffic with a heavy vehicle, one of these is a smart thing to remember:

    A. In traffic, heavy vehicles require wider gaps than cars.

B. Pulling the car partway across the road and blocking one lane while waiting for another to clear is the safest way to cross traffic.

C. Since heavy vehicles are easy to see, other drivers will count on you to move out of your way to slow down.

60. Which of these claims is true for those kinds of cargo?

A. Unstable loads may require extra caution on curves, such as hanging meat or livestock.

B. During periods when the roads are not busy, oversize loads may be hauled without special permits.

C. The tank should still be fully loaded while liquids are transported.

61. Which of these claims is true about acceleration?

A. Mechanical damage can be caused by rough acceleration.

B. If you do a proper accelerator of your engine, you can experience a "jerking" motion.

C. More power should be added to the accelerator when traction is low.

62. Which of these statements is true about remaining alert to drive?

A. A coffee break for half an hour would do more to keep you alert than a nap for half an hour.

B. Drugs that can cure exhaustion are available.

C. The single thing that can conquer exhaustion is sleep.

63. Holding the load is a crucial concept to note about loading cargo:

A. Towards the front.

B. Towards the rear.

C. In the cargo field, balanced.

64. Which of these is a positive thing to remember for mirror use?

A. You are supposed to see a mirror for a few seconds at a time.

B. Convex mirrors make the stuff look bigger and closer than it is.

C. There are "blind spots" that cannot be shown to you by your mirror.

65. At 50 mph, you're driving on a straight, level road. In front of you, there are no cars. A tire suddenly blows down on your vehicle. First, what should you do?

A. Steer towards the driver's side easily.

B. Start braking for emergencies.

C. Keep the brakes off until the car has slowed down.

66. You are driving on a two-lane road. An oncoming driver is driving into your lane and heading for you straight away. Which of these is the right step to take more often?

  A. Hard brake.

  B. Steer to the right.

  C. Steer toward your left shoulder.

67. You're driving a manual transmission truck. When driving on a grade uphill, you have to stop the truck on your side. Which of these is a reasonable rule to be followed when the truck is put back in motion?

  A. While slowly accelerating, keep the clutch slipping.

  B. To hold the vehicle until the clutch engages, use the parking brake.

  C. Before you engage the clutch, let the vehicle roll straight back a few feet.

68. Your vehicle has hydraulic brakes. You click the brake pedal while traveling on a level road and notice that it goes to the floor. Which of these arguments is the truth?

  A. If you have an automatic transmission, you should not downshift.

  B. Pumping the brake pedal can increase the pressure so that the vehicle can be stopped.

  C. Even because it is part of the same hydraulic system, the parking brake will not work.

  69. A vehicle is loaded with most of the weight on the steering axle. What might be the result?

  A. Hard steering and potential tire damage.

  B. Improved handling.

  C. Too little traction on the steering axle.

70. "Fade" Brake:

  A. Very hot brakes can trigger it.

  B. It can be corrected within one to two seconds of letting up on the brakes and then putting them on again.

  C. It's an issue that only happens with drum brakes.

71. At 50 mph, you're driving a 40-foot truck. Driving conditions (dry pavement, decent visibility) are perfect. What is the minimum amount of safe space you can hold in front of your vehicle?

  A. Three seconds.

  B. Four seconds.

  C. Five seconds.

72. Which of these motor overheating claims is true?

   A. If your engine overheats within 20 miles of the end of your journey, the trip should be completed and the problem tested.

   B. When it cools, you can never switch off an overheated engine.

   C. Once the system has cooled, you can never remove the radiator cap on a pressurized system.

73. On your Commercial Driver's License, you should not have a Hazardous Materials Endorsement. You are invited to deliver unsafe products in a placarded truck. Should you:

   A. Refusing to bear the load.

   B. Take off the truck with the placards.

   C. Haul the load, but only to the nearest location where a driver with a Hazardous Materials Endorsement may take over.

74. You need to stop driving:

   A. Five hours after that.

   B. Nine hours after that.

   C. Whenever you make yourself sleepy.

75. When steering to stop a collision, which of these is a safe thing to do?

   A. When turning, apply the brakes.

   B. Steer with one hand so that you can turn the wheel faster.

   C. To explain what is in your direction, do not turn any more than required.

76. Which of these steps will help keep your brakes working if you have to drive through deep puddles or running water?

   A. Rapidly driving along.

   B. Put on the brakes gently when driving through the water.

   C. After getting out of the water, apply firm pressure on both the brake pedal and accelerator.

77. For a pre-trip inspection, you check your wheels and rims. Which of these arguments is the truth?

   A. Rust around the nuts of the wheel may mean they are loose.

   B. It is possible to use cracked wheels or rims if they have been welded.

   C. With one missing lug nut on a wheel, a vehicle can be safely driven.

78. What happens as the concentration of blood alcohol (BAC) goes up?

A. The drinker sees more clearly how they are influenced by alcohol.

B. It affects judgment and self-control.

C. In less time, the drinker will sober up.

79. In a traffic emergency, if you need to leave the lane, you should:

    A. Try separating all the wheels from the pavement.

    B. As you leave the lane, brake hard.

    C. Stop braking until your speed has fallen to around 20 mph.

80. Which of these claims about a long downhill grade downshift is true?

    A. For automatic transmissions, it should not be achieved.

    B. To help slow the car, it enables engine compression and friction.

    C. The proper time to downshift is just after the vehicle starts down the slope.

81. Which of these cold-weather driving claims are true?

    A. When the weather is very cold, an engine will overheat.

    B. An antifreeze windshield washer should be used.

    C. In cold weather, exhaust system leaks are less harmful.

82. Braking controlled:

    A. It can be used when you turn sharply.

    B. It includes the wheels being locked for brief periods.

    C. When braking, it is used to keep a vehicle in a straight line.

83. While looking in front of your vehicle when driving, you should watch:

    A. To the side of the road on the right.

    B. To the lane on the left.

    C. Back and forth, close and far.

84. When caring for wounded people at an accident scene, one of these is not a reasonable law to follow:

    A. If eligible individuals are assisting them, stay out of the way unless requested to assist.

    B. Keep injured individuals in calm.

    C. If there is a risk due to fire or moving traffic, transfer critically injured individuals.

85. Ramps for escape are:

    A. Used for stopping a speeding driver.

    B. Just for tankers.

C. Only for combination vehicles.

86. While driving at night, you should:

   A. To maintain your stopping distance within your viewing distance, change your velocity.

   B. Look on the left side of the road as you are approached by a car.

   C. When your low beams are on, drive quicker.

87. When setting up reflective triangles for your defense, you should:

   A. Bear the triangles on your hand.

   B. Keep the triangles between yourself and oncoming traffic.

   C. While you walk to the spots where you put them up, keep them out of view.

88. When are you expected to wear seatbelts?

   A. You're in a moving car at any moment.

   B. Only in jurisdictions where the legislation allows it.

   C. Only when engaged in interstate trade.

89. How do you correct an accelerated skid on the rear-wheel?

   A. Apply the wheels with more power.

   B. Stop the acceleration.

   C. Apply the brakes.

90. Which of these claims are valid about vehicle fires?

   A. You can open the freight doors as soon as you can if the freight in a van or a box trailer catches on fire.

   B. You can open the hood as soon as you can if your engine is on fire.

   C. It is sufficient to cool a burning tire with water.

91. Hydro planning:

   A. It only takes place at speeds above 50 mph.

   B. It can't happen while driving through a puddle.

   C. If the tire pressure is low, this is more probable.

92. Which of these claims is accurate about overhead clearance?

   A. You should believe that the clearance signs displayed are correct.

   B. A vehicle's weight alters its height.

   C. You can drive near the driver's side if the road surface causes your vehicle to tip toward objects at the edge of the road.

93. Severe vehicle skids are most frequently triggered by:

    A. Too hard moving for road conditions.

    B. Poorly tailored brakes.

    C. Bad tires.

94. Which of these, when using a fire extinguisher, is a safe law to follow?

    A. Keep it as close as possible to the flames.

    B. Keep with the fire downwind.

    C. Target at the base of the fire.

95. Heavy vehicles tend to drive more slowly than other traffic at times. When you are driving such a car, one of these is not a reasonable rule to follow:

    A. Signal to other drivers to pass you when it is safe for them.

    B. Keep on your right.

    C. If it is legal to do so, switching on the flashers.

96. It is necessary to test the parking brake when the vehicle is:

    A. Parked.

    B. Slowly going forwards.

    C. Going downhill.

97. This is the most significant explanation for being alert to hazards:

    A. The accident reports would be specific.

    B. Personnel from law enforcement can be called.

    C. If the threat becomes an emergency, you will have time to plan your escape.

98. If you're tailgating, you should:

    A. Increase the gap that follows.

    B. Flash the lights on the brakes.

    C. Signal the tailgater to pass you when it is clear.

Left Turn Diagram
(For Use With Question 99)

99. Refer to the figure above this question. You're driving a long truck, a long one that makes big turns. You want to turn left onto Cedar Street from Pine Street. Both are streets that are two-lane, two-way. Should you:

   A. As soon as you can reach the junction, start turning your vehicle around.

   B. Start the turn in the left lane of Pine Street in your car.

   C. When you are halfway through the intersection, start turning your vehicle around.

100. You see a small (one-foot-square) cardboard box ahead of you in your lane when driving. Should you:

   A. Without making a sudden or risky move, steer around it.

   B. To stop reaching it, brake hard.

   C. To knock it off the lane, hit it with your car.

AIR BRAKES PRACTICE TEST

Instructor: _____   Class: _____

_____

Name: _____   Date: _____

1. It takes more time for air braking than for hydraulic braking because:

    A. The brakes use multiple brake drums.

    B. Takes more time than hydraulic fluid to flow through the lines.

    C. Airline fittings still leak through.

2. Three separate systems include advanced air brake systems. They are the operation system, the parking system, and the:

    A. Emergency braking system.

    B. Footing system.

    C. Drum system.

3. If there are dual parking control valves in your vehicle, you can use pressure from a separate tank to:

    A. Release the spring emergency parking brakes to drive a short distance.

    B. Add more brake pressure if the main tank is getting smaller.

    C. Keep parked with your service air pressure for twice as long.

4. The driver needs to see a signal before air pressure falls below _____ psi in the service air tanks.

    A. 40.

    B. 60.

    C. 80.

5. In an air brake system, the brake pedal:

    A. Regulates the air compressor's speed.

    B. Is often best to keep it halfway down during normal driving.

    C. Controls the pressure of air applied to the brakes.

6. If an alcohol evaporator is in your car, it is there to:

    A. Get rid of a wet alcohol tank that condenses and rests at the bottom of the tank.

    B. Eliminate the need for regular draining of tanks.

    C. Reduce the risk in cold weather of ice in air brake valves.

7. All air brake-equipped vehicles have:

    A. A hydraulic system in the event of an air system falling.

    B. A pressure gauge of supply.

    C. A gauge of air use.

8. How often should you drain the oil and water from the bottom of compressed air storage tanks if you do not have automatic tank drains?

    A. At the end of a single driving day.

    B. Once a week.

    C. Every other week.

9. To verify the free play of manual slack adjusters on S-cam brakes, park on:

    A. With the parking brake on, level the field, then apply the service brake.

    B. Chock the wheels, level the ground, and release the parking brake.

    C. Level the field and drain before changing the air pressure.

10. Of the following options, the first thing to do when an alert of low air pressure comes on is:

    A. Stop and park comfortably as soon as possible.

    B. Shift to a higher gear next.

    C. Open the valve for air supply control.

11. If you have to stop in an emergency, brake so that you:

    A. Use the brakes' full power and lock them.

B. Your vehicle remains in a straight line and can steer.

C. Use the hand-brake first.

12. The governor's air compressor controls:

    A. As pressures the brake chambers release.

    B. The air pressure on the brakes.

    C. If the air in the air tanks is pumped.

13. The braking strength of the brakes in the spring:

    A. The operation does not impair the state of the brakes.

    B. Only highly trained brake service personnel can be tested.

    C. It depends on whether there are modifications to the service brakes.

14. Every day during cold weather, if your vehicle has an alcohol evaporator, you should:

    A. Check the alcohol level and, if appropriate, fill in the evaporator.

    B. Shift the alcohol.

    C. Disinfect the air filter with alcohol.

15. Spring brakes are normally kept back during regular driving by:

    A. Clamps or bolts.

    B. Air pressure.

    C. Spring pressure.

16. The pressure gauge for the application indicates how much air pressure you need to:

    A. Use on this trip.

    B. Get by your air tank.

    C. Apply to the brakes.

17. Parking brakes can be used in air brake vehicles:

    A. About as few as possible.

    B. The car will be parked at all times.

    C. To maintain your pace as you go downhill.

18. Your brakes fade when:

    A. You must press harder on the brake pedal to control your speed on a downgrade.

    B. When you apply pressure, the brake pedal feels spongy.

    C. You release pressure and speed increases on the brake pedal.

19. Why is it that you must drain water from compressed air tanks?

A. The low boiling point of water limits braking strength.

B. In cold weather, water can freeze and cause brake failure.

C. To keep the oil of an air compressor clean.

20. There is a dual air braking system in your car. If a low air pressure alert comes on for the secondary system, you should:

A. Bring the car to a safe stop and then proceed when the machine is fixed.

B. Reduce your rpm and, while driving, measure the rest of the system.

C. Reduce your rpm and drive for repairs to the nearest garage.

21. For a straight truck with the engine off and the brakes on, the air loss rate should be no more than:

A. In 30 seconds, one psi.

B. Two psi in 45 seconds.

C. In one minute, three psi.

22. When the driver uses the brake lever, the brake mechanism that applies and activates the brakes is the brake:

A. Service.

B. Parking.

C. Drum.

23. Emergency stab braking is when you do:

A. Push the brake pedal hard and fully apply the hand valve before you stop.

B. For one second, apply the hand valve, then press hard on the accelerator.

C. Brake as hard as you can; when the wheels lock, remove the brake, and put on the brakes again when the wheels start to roll.

24. With the engine off and the brakes released, a straight truck air brake scheme does not leak at a rate greater than _____ psi per minute.

A. Six.

B. Four.

C. Two.

25. Give time for the air compressor to produce a minimum before starting a car with a dual air device. In both the primary and secondary systems, _____ psi strain.

A. 25

B. 50

C. 100

26. How much pressure the supply pressure gauge indicates:

A. You used it on that bus.

B. It's inside the air tanks.

C. That goes to the brake chambers.

27. Which of these makes the total stopping distance longer than the hydraulic brakes for air brakes?

A. Lag of brakes.

B. Distance from experience.

C. Distance for reaction time.

28. Due to the altitude, the overall stopping distance for air brakes is longer than for hydraulic brakes.

A. Perception.

B. The reaction.

C. Brake lag.

29. What stops the air in the tank if the air compressor develops a leak?

A. The one-way valve for testing.

B. The valve of the emergency relay.

C. The safety valve for the tractor.

30. The most popular form of base brake that is used on heavy vehicles is:

A. Brake disc.

B. Wedge brake drum.

C. Drum brake S-cam.

COMBINATION VEHICLES PRACTICE TEST

Directions: The questions are about driving combination vehicles safely during this test. If you want to drive a combination truck, such as a semi-trailer tractor, double trailer rig, or triple trailer rig, you must pass this test.

For each question, there is only one correct answer. Respond to all questions. On the answer sheet given, mark your answer.

1. Before you go back under the trailer, make sure that the:

 A. Trailer brakes are locked.

 B. The valve for tractor safety is natural.

 C. The air brakes are already off.

2. You are coupled to a semi-trailer by a tractor and have backed up but are not under it. What do you need to hook up under before backing up?

 A. The cable for electrical service.

 B. Emergency air line and service lines.

 C. Nothing: back up and lock the wheel on the sixth.

3. You cannot back up a tractor under a trailer until the whole air system is:

 A. At normal pressure.

 B. Bled down to a maximum pressure of half.

 C. About sixty and eighty psi.

4. You should line up as you get ready to go back under the semi-trailer.

 A. Approximately 12 degrees off the trailer side.

 B. The kingpin must first engage the driver's side locking jaw.

C. In front of the trailer, directly.

5. You're attaching a semi-trailer to your tractor, but you haven't backed down yet. The trailer is positioned at the correct height when:

   A. The kingpin is around 1 1/4 inches above the fifth wheel.

   B. The end of the kingpin is even with the top of the fifth wheel.

   C. It will be lifted slightly when the tractor is supported under it.

6. How do you test the semi-trailer link of the tractor for safety?

   A. Place the tractor in gear and pull a sharp jerk forward.

   B. In low gear, pull gently forward against the locked trailer brakes. Look at it closely then.

   C. With the trailer brakes closed, you rock the trailer back and forth.

7. If you are driving a mixed car, the servicing air line falls off, but the emergency line remains together. What will happen right away?

   A. The brakes for the emergency tractor will come on.

   B. The air tank of the trailer will exhaust it across the open line.

   C. Until you attempt to apply the brakes, nothing is likely to happen.

8. What part of the kingpin are the locking jaws expected to close around?

   A. The shank.

   B. The head of it.

   C. The foundation.

9. When do you park a combination vehicle using the hand valve?

   A. To park at docks for loading.

   B. To park on a grade.

   C. Never.

10. After the jaws close around the kingpin, the fifth wheel locking lever is not closed. This implies that:

   A. You can set the fifth wheel to balance your weight.

   B. The lock-in the parking lot is off, and you can drive away.

   C. The coupling is not accurate and should be corrected before the linked unit is powered.

11. For a combination vehicle (engine off, brakes on), the air leakage rate should be less than _____ psi per minute.

A. Two.

B. Three.

C. Four.

12. To the trailer tanks, you supply air through:

    A. Pushing in the air supply valve for the trailer.

    B. Pulling out the air supply valve for the trailer.

    C. Connecting a glad-hand to the service line.

13. You have a combined semi-trailer. Before driving forward, what place do you put the front trailer support/landing gear in?

    A. Raised halfway with the handle of the crank cut.

    B. Completely elevated in its bracket with the crank handle secured.

    C. With the crank handle locked in its bracket and the top shut off three times.

14. Some drivers use the hand valve in regular driving to stop a jackknife before applying the brake pedal. Which of these are the real statements?

    A. It ought not to be done.

    B. This leads to less skidding than using the brake pedal by itself.

    C. That is the safest way to hold the truck in a straight line and brake.

15. A combination vehicle's air leakage rate (engine off, brakes off) should be less than ____ psi per minute.

    A. One.

    B. Two.

    C. Three.

16. Why should you be sure that, as needed, the fifth wheel plate is greased?

    A. To guarantee excellent electrical connections.

    B. To avoid issues with steering.

    C. To decrease noise and heat.

17. When hooking up to an old trailer, a driver crossed the air lines. What's going to happen?

    A. If there are no spring brakes on the trailer, you can drive away, but you won't have any trailer brakes.

    B. Rather than the trailer brakes, the hand valve will apply the tractor brakes.

C. The brake pedal operates instead of the air brakes on the trailer spring brakes.

18. To prevent them from being mixed up, air lines on a hybrid vehicle are also colored. The line for emergencies is:

   A. Red, blue.

   B. Black, yellow.

   C. Blue, red.

19. To avoid a rollover, there are two things that a driver should do. They are: (1) hold the cargo as near to the ground as possible, and (2):

   A. Make sure the brakes are calibrated properly.

   B. Go round the turns slowly.

   C. Keep the free play of the fifth wheel as strict as possible.

20. Make sure the air lines are not crossed and the trailer brakes operate after you supply air to the trailer. Do you do this?

   A. Turning on the cab's parking brakes.

   B. The trailer brakes are applied and released, and brake sounds are listened to.

   C. Raising the pedal for the brake.

21. Semi-trailers made before 1975 that are equipped with air brakes:

   A. Since they are heavier, stopping is simpler.

   B. A glad-hand converter is typically required.

   C. Often, spring brakes are not available.

22. Which of these arguments is the truth?

   A. Braking a heavy vehicle is often delayed until you have no other choice.

   B. Light vehicles need more stopping power than heavy ones to stop.

   C. It can take longer to stop the "Bobtail" tractors than a combination vehicle filled to the full gross weight.

23. If you are not towing a trailer, why should you lock the tractors glad-hands (or dummy couplers) to one another?

   A. A backup air tank becomes the associated brake circuit.

   B. It's going to keep dirt and water away from the row.

   C. You would never be able to create machine pressure if you did not.

24. A tractor and a semi-trailer are connected, and the air lines are connected. Before backing up under the trailer, you should:

   A. Supply the trailer machine with air, then take the air supply knob out of it to secure the trailer brakes.

   B. Ensure that the brakes on the trailer are off.

   C. To warn others, apply the brakes twice.

25. It is worth using the hand valve:

   A. Just with a brake on your foot.

   B. To test the brakes on the trailer.

   C. Only when fully loaded with the trailer.

26. To complete a coupling, the safety catch for the fifth wheel locking lever must be:

   A. Via the locking lever.

   B. Under the locking lever.

   C. Above the locking lever.

27. The support/landing gear of the front trailer is up, and the trailer is sitting on the tractor. Ensure that:

   A. Between the tops of the tractor tires and the trailer nose, there is ample clearance.

   B. Between the tractor frame and the landing gear, there is ample clearance.

   C. A and B are both right.

28. When you are driving, your emergency air line breaks or gets ripped apart. The loss of pressure will trigger:

   A. Emergency brakes for the trailer to get on.

   B. Air compressor for unloading instead of air pumping.

   C. The trailer supply valve to open.

29. In the service line, you have a big leak, and you put the brakes on.

   A. Emergency trailer brakes to come on.

   B. The pressure of the trailer tank will be lost.

   C. Spring brakes for tractors to lock on.

30. You are driving a hybrid truck when the trailer breaks free, pulling all air lines apart. You'd expect:

113

A. To lose all the air pressure on the tractor.

B. Closing the tractor safety valve.

C. A trailer supply valve to remain open.

31. You're about to bring your tractor back under the semi-trailer. When is the trailer at the right height?

A. The landing gear trailer is fully extended.

B. Even the top of the fifth wheel is at the end of the kingpin.

C. When the tractor backs under it, the trailer will be slightly raised.

32. After coupling, how much space should there be between the upper and the lower fifth wheel?

A. Half an inch, at least.

B. Nothing.

C. Only enough to get through it to see the light.

HAZARDOUS MATERIALS PRACTICE TEST

1. A hazardous material placarded vehicle must have _____ placards on the doors.

    A. Two.

    B. Three.

    C. Four.

2. You are behind the wheel of a truck transporting a hazardous material shipment. The shipping papers must be on the driver's door in a pouch or in:

    A. A box under the seat of the driver.

    B. Clear view within reach of you.

    C. The glove box of the truck.

3. Who is responsible for figuring out what permits or special routes you're going to need to move dangerous materials?

    A. Driver.

    B. Carriers.

    C. Shipper.

4. Who is responsible for the packaging, marking, and planning for a particular carrier of hazardous material shipping documents?

    A. Shipper.

    B. Carriers.

    C. Driver.

5. To determine whether a material is a regulated commodity, there are two specified lists that drivers, shippers, and carriers use. Is it one of these lists?

A. List of Hazardous Substances and Reportable Quantities.

B. EPA Hazardous Materials Table.

C. Shippers list of transportable quantities.

6. NO ONE can smoke at a distance of 25 feet from any vehicle containing explosives, oxidizers, or:

   A. Toxins.

   B. Materials that are flammable.

   C. Gases that are compressed.

7. When an X or an RQ is in the "HM" column of a shipping paper, entry:

   A. The largest portion of the shipment is the material listed on that line.

   B. This refers to the materials that need to be loaded on top.

   C. Shipment is regulated by hazardous material regulations.

8. Only one of these descriptions of shipping paper for hazardous material is in the correct order. Which is this one?

   A. Corrosive material, UN 1789, Hydrochloric acid.

   B. Non-flammable steam, Hydrogen Bromide, UN 10488.

   C. Hexane, UN 1208, flammable liquid.

9. Another vehicle crashed into a truck carrying explosives. They should not be taken apart until:

   A. The loading foreman for the shipper is present.

   B. Vehicles and inhabited buildings were positioned at least 200 feet away from the explosives.

   C. 30 minutes have gone, at least.

10. You should not park a vehicle containing dangerous materials within _____ feet of an open fire.

    A. 100.

    B. 200.

    C. 300.

11. Index of the transport of radioactive material:

    A. This is another way to write down the package's weight.

    B. Indicate the degree of control required during transport.

    C. It's something the shipper just has to think about.

12. When dangerous materials are transported, the car must be stopped, and any dual tires must be tested at least once every:

    A. One hour or 50 miles.

    B. Two hours or 100 miles.

    C. Three hours or 150 miles.

13. You can stop _____ feet before the nearest track to stop for railroad trails.

    A. Five to 20.

    B. Around ten to 35.

    C. 15 to 50.

14. You carry toxic materials. If you are not behind the wheel, the shipping documents must be on the seat of the driver or:

    A. On the driver's door in the pouch.

    B. With you.

    C. In plain view on the dashboard.

15. If dangerous materials leak from your car, do not move your car:

    A. More than 500 feet in total.

    B. Toward the upwind.

    C. Any more than safety requires.

16. You will be moving dangerous materials along a path that you do not know well. When do you check the route and obtain the requisite permits for this trip?

    A. Until the trip begins.

    B. When you are already on a section of the path that you are familiar with.

    C. 24 hours after the conclusion of the journey.

17. Carriers must supply each driver carrying explosives in Class A or B with:

    A. An additional bottle of flames.

    B. Phone number of the consignee.

    C. A copy of part 397 of the Federal Motor Carrier Safety Regulations (FMCSR).

18. You can stop before crossing a railroad grade if your vehicle is carrying _____ of chlorine:

    A. Ten gallons.

B. 100 gallons.

C. Any quantity.

19. You are carrying toxic goods, and you learn that one of your tires leaks. You're supposed to:

    A. Continue at a reduced pace, and every 25 miles, check the tire.

    B. Stop at the safe place nearest you and repair it.

    C. Immediately report it to your carrier.

20. When shippers package hazardous materials, they must certify that this has been achieved according to the legislation. The only exception would be when:

    A. The shipper is a private carrier delivering a commodity of its own.

    B. This shipment is a dangerous waste.

    C. A sealed cargo compartment is provided to the driver.

21. While powering a placarded vehicle, someone has to be:

    A. Within ten feet of a fire extinguisher pump.

    B. Controlling the fuel flow at the nozzle.

    C. A power shut-off for the pump in an emergency.

22. Animals and human foodstuffs in the same car should not be filled with:

    A. Toxins.

    B. Gases of Flammable.

    C. Explosives.

23. In the last _____ years, a driver who carries radioactive materials and has to follow a certain direction must have had special training from the carrier.

    A. Two.

    B. Three.

    C. Four.

24. Do not drive near open fires anytime your vehicle is placarded unless you:

    A. Are outfitted with fire sprinklers.

    B. Have a non-flammable material with LTL.

    C. You can easily pass through the fire without stopping.

25. When there is an emergency with hazardous materials, you should:

    A. Keep people away, and caution them about risk.

B. Prevent smoking and stay away from open flames.

C. Do the above all.

26. What signals can be used to warn of an explosive-containing vehicle being stopped?

    A. Signal fires.

    B. Triangles Reflective.

    C. With flares or fuses.

27. When storing chlorine in cargo tanks, you must have:

    A. An approved mask for the gas.

    B. An emergency kit to control leaks on the dome cover plate in the fittings.

    C. A and B both.

28. If the term "Forbidden" appears in the hazard column of an entry in the table of hazardous materials:

    A. A common carrier must never carry away the content.

    B. There must never be a shipment of that content greater than the RQ.

    C. The package or container could not be opened by the carrier.

29. When handling explosive packages, you need:

    A. Never use hooks or other tools made of metal.

    B. Hold 100 meters away from the bystanders.

    C. To avoid staining, double cover wet boxes in plastic.

30. A railroad crossing is ahead of you, and you handle dangerous material. You will stop as far as _____ feet from the nearest rail as you stop for the crossing.

    A. 25.

    B. 50.

    C. 75.

31. Who is responsible for safely moving a dangerous material shipment without delay and keeping the shipping documents in the right place?

    A. The driver.

    B. The carrier.

    C. The shipper.

32. A hazardous material's basic definition includes the hazard class, the ID Number, and the proper name for shipping. Which one on the shipping paper needs to appear first?

A. The hazard class.

B. The proper name for shipping.

C. The number of identification.

33. Explosives of class A shall not be transported in a combination vehicle, provided that the vehicle includes:

A. Two trailers or more.

B. A trailer with a 200-inch wheelbase.

C. A placarded tank of cargo.

34. During an en-route check, you notice an overheated tire. If you're transporting dangerous items, you must:

A. Before continuing your journey, wait at least two hours.

B. Cool the pneumatic tire, then test it every two hours.

C. Remove the tire from the vehicle and position it a safe distance away.

35. The placarded vehicle's power unit must have a fire extinguisher with a UL ranking of:

A. Five.

B. Ten.

C. 15.

36. A fully prepared Manifesto of Uniform Hazardous Waste:

A. Must be signed and hold it by anyone transporting hazardous waste.

B. Is the same as all other shipping papers.

C. Is only important if there is a loss of cargo during transport.

37. For most hazardous materials, if your job needs it, you can briefly park within five feet of the lane. The materials that are the exception and do not allow this close to the road for parking are:

A. A and B explosives.

B. Oxidizers and corrosives.

C. Poisons and acids.

38. The purpose of the regulations on hazardous materials is to ensure protection, to contain the material, and:

A. To correctly tax shippers.

B. To make the danger known.

C. To allow state compliance.

39. To find out if dangerous materials are included in a shipment, you must:

   A. Open every box and container and inspect them.

   B. Check around the loading dock for a fence.

   C. Look at the documents for delivery.

40. To carry cylinders or compressed gas, you have a vehicle without shelves. You are only permitted to load those cylinders if they are:

   A. Loaded upright, flat, and braced to lay down.

   B. Bundled loosely with steel strapping together.

   C. With less than half the load.

41. A vehicle contains 500 pounds of explosives A and B. You've got to have:

   A. Placards "Explosives A."

   B. "Dangerous" placards.

   C. Placards of "Blasting Agents."

42. An X in the HM column of a shipping paper entry means:

   A. The substance does not constitute a hazardous material.

   B. This is an exception to the Rules on Hazardous Materials.

   C. The entry is for harmful material.

43. Which of the following must be in drivers' hands while transporting Class A or B explosives?

   A. The insurance policy of the carrier.

   B. The published plan of the route.

   C. Both of the latter.

44. The cumulative transport index in a single-vehicle of all packages of radioactive material shall not exceed.

   A. Ten.

   B. 50.

   C. 100.

45. Who is responsible for checking to make sure a hazardous materials shipment is appropriately called, numbered, and labeled by the shipper?

   A. The shipper.

   B. The manufacturer.

C. The carriers.

46. If it has an RQ before or after the description of the item on the shipping sheet, it means:

    A. The insurance value of the equipment is over $1,000.00.

    B. The content is in a box that does not contain any other materials.

    C. Any spill of this material must be announced by the carrier.

47. A toxic material has been loaded into a cargo tank. What do you need to do before the vehicle moves?

    A. By phone, call Chemical Transportation Emergency Center (CHEMTREC) and tell them where you are headed.

    B. Have the shipping papers signed by the loading observers.

    C. Close all valves and manholes. Make sure they're leak-free.

48. You cannot identify a hazardous class name or ID number as:

    A. Non-hazardous substance.

    B. The reportable volume of a toxic drug.

    C. Hazardous residue.

49. If you are in an accident involving hazardous materials, you should:

    A. Only notify the emergency response team about the threat.

    B. Keep all the people far away from the crash and upwind.

    C. Avoid the panic by behaving like nothing is wrong.

50. On your Commercial Driver's License, you should not have a Hazardous Materials endorsement. When can you legally move unsafe materials?

    A. If it is a non-placarded material, only.

    B. Only when placarding the load.

    C. Only when the shipment does not cross the lines of the territory.

TANKER VEHICLES PRACTICE TEST

Directions: The Tank Vehicles Test examines what a driver needs to know to drive tanker trucks safely. To receive a tanker endorsement on your CDL, you must pass the Tank Vehicles Test. To pass this written information test, your state will possibly require you to answer 80 percent of the questions correctly.

The questions for your practice are about this exam. They are close to the questions on the test for your state.

1. Side-to-side surges can result in:

    A. Suspension failure of the system.

    B. Over speeding.

    C. A rollover.

2. What does a liquid surge do to a tanker's handling?

    A. Increases the drag of the truck's wind.

    B. It can drive the truck in the direction of the movement of liquid waves.

    C. Let's you turn tighter corners.

3. Hauling liquids in tankers take special care because of.

    A. Flat.

    B. Wide.

    C. High.

4. How would you expect a truck with a cargo tank on the road to treat baffles?

    A. The truck is going to look bigger than it is.

    B. There is going to be less front-to-back surge than there is in a baffle-free tanker.

    C. The truck can handle the same thing as a baffle-free tanker.

5. When running smooth bore tankers, you need to be very vigilant. This is particularly true when you are:

A. Starting or halting.

B. Loading and unloading.

C. Hauling milk or other foodstuffs.

6. Empty lorries:

   A. When you just use the emergency brake or parking brake, stop sooner.

   B. Have more traction than full trucks while braking.

   C. A longer stopping distance than full trucks can be required.

7. When you discharge the smaller tans of a bulkhead tank, be careful to verify your:

   A. Weight distribution.

   B. Air ratio to gasoline.

   C. Containing water.

8. Before hitting the curve, the safest way to take a curve with a tanker is to slow to a reasonable pace, then_____ as you go through it.

   A. Speed up slightly.

   B. Lightly brake.

   C. Downshift twice.

9. What kind of surge can the fluid in a tank with baffles have?

   A. Side-to-the-side.

   B. Top-to-the-bottom.

   C. Front-to-back.

10. When operating smooth bore tankers, you should be very careful, especially when you are:

   A. Heading downhill or uphill.

   B. Starting or halting.

   C. Driving against the storm.

11. The outage needed for the liquids you are carrying should be known because:

   A. No outage is expected for some of the heavier liquids.

   B. Tank baffles with an outage are not always legal.

   C. When they get warm, some liquids expand more than others.

12. If the small tanks of a cargo tank fitted with bulkheads are filled, you can check:

   A. Containing water.

   B. Air ratio to gasoline.

C. Weight distribution.

13. Baffles do not normally avoid _____ spikes in liquid cargo tanks.

    A. Side-to-the-side.

    B. Top-to-the-bottom.

    C. Front-to-back.

14. You're driving on a clear night. Your headlights must be dimmed from high to low. You need to change your speed so you can stop until:

    A. The distance you are going to move in the next 15 seconds.

    B. You can see the gap ahead.

    C. Your vehicle's duration.

15. What handling impact do you expect when your cargo tank has defects?

    A. There's going to be a smaller side-to-side surge than there is in a baffle-free tank.

    B. There's going to be less surge from front-to-back than there is for a tank.

    C. There is going to be a slower surge than a quick one.

16. Hauling liquids in tank vehicles take special care because:

    A. Movement of liquids.

    B. Extreme gravity.

    C. Expansion unevenly.

17. When can a truck escape ramp be used by the driver of a tanker which has lost its brakes?

    A. Only when there are baffles in the tank.

    B. Always.

    C. Never.

18. You are driving a tanker truck, and the front wheels are starting to skid. Which one of these is most likely to take place?

    A. No matter how you steer, you will continue in a straight line and keep moving forward.

    B. The tank will be pulled from the truck by the liquid surge.

    C. It'll roll the truck over.

19. An emergency forces you to swiftly stop or crash your tanker. Should you:

    A. Lock the pedal on the brakes and leave it there.

    B. Use the emergency brakes only.

    C. Apply regulated braking or stab braking.

20. Which of these emergency steering and tanker claims is true?

    A. A tanker can be counter-steered more quickly than other cars.

B. Using the emergency brakes only.

C. Before performing a fast steering movement, you can wrap your thumbs around the steering wheel.

21. Outage implies:

A. Liquid weight.

B. How easily it drains the liquid tanks.

C. Allowance for liquid expansion.

22. Within tanks, liquid-tight separators between compartments are called:

A. Bulkheads.

B. Baffles.

C. Barriers.

23. The quantity of liquid to be loaded into the tank will depend on:

A. The volume of liquid can expand in transit.

B. The limits of legal weight.

C. Both of the considerations above.

24. Separators that are between compartments in a tank, with gaps or holes in them, are called:

A. Bulkheads.

B. Baffles.

C. Barriers.

25. Which of these stopping distance and velocity statements are true?

A. At 40 mph, you need about two times as many stopping distances as at 20 mph.

B. Wet roads can, at any speed, double the stopping distance.

C. The above are both real.

This completes the Practice Evaluation of Tank Vehicles. Have you replied to all 25 questions? The tanker test in your state would likely include 15 to 20 related questions.

DOUBLES/TRIPLES PRACTICE TEST

Directions: The questions for your practice are about this exam. They are close to the questions that your state is going to ask you. To earn the endorsement on your CDL, you must pass the Doubles/Triples Test. This is a measure of the skills needed to drive double and triple trailer units safely.

1. What trailer should be the first one behind the tractor while traveling with more than one trailer?

    A. The shortest trailer.

    B. The heaviest trailer.

    C. The lightest trailer.

2. Which of these claims is accurate about fast steering movements and doubles/ triples?

    A. More quickly than many other cars, doubles/triples flip over from fast steering motions.

    B. You can put on the brakes at the same time as you execute rapid steering motions.

    C. For doubles/triples, counter-steering is simpler than with most other cars.

3. You drive a 100-foot twin trailer combination at 50 mph. The road is dry, and there is decent visibility. You should keep space ahead of you for at least ____ seconds.

    A. Nine.

    B. Ten.

    C. 11.

4. Before attaching a convertor dolly to the second or third trailer, you must check the trailer's height. The height of the trailer is correct when:

    A. The trailer will be lifted slightly when the convertor dolly is supported under it.

    B. The core of the kingpin lines up with the locking jaws.

    C. The kingpin lies on the fifth wheel.

5. You're driving a 100-foot truck with dual trailers at 30 mph. The road is dry, and there is decent visibility. You should keep space ahead of you for at least ____ seconds.

    A. Nine.

B. Ten.

C. 11.

6. You can test the trailer brakes with the hand valve on by opening the service line valve at the rear of the truck. You can hear it when you do this:

   A. Open and expel air through the emergency line valve.

   B. Service brakes slowly shift to the location that is completely applied.

   C. Air spills out of an open valve.

7. Empty lorries:

   A. Shorter stopping distances are required than complete ones.

   B. May have weak tractions due to bouncing and wheel lockup.

   C. Since there's no moving freight, they are the simplest to avoid.

8. When driving on slippery roads, which one of these is not a smart thing to do?

   A. Use the speed retarder or engine brake.

   B. Keep other traffic out of the room on your side.

   C. On the accelerator and brake pedals, use a gentle touch.

9. Which of these declarations is true about treating doubles and triples?

   A. Due to off-tracking, a triple bottom rig can stop faster than a five-axle tractor semi-trailer.

   B. Due to the crack-the-whip effect, the rear trailer of a 100-foot triple is less likely to turn over than a single semi-trailer.

   C. A sudden steering wheel movement may result in a rear trailer tipping over.

10. Before you can supply air to a second trailer's air tanks, you need to:

    A. Close the shut-off valves at the rear of both trailers.

    B. Open the shut-off valves at the rear of both trailers.

    C. Open the shut-off valves at the rear of the first trailer and close the shut-off valves at the rear of the second trailer.

11. You're driving a double trailer, and you need to use your brakes to prevent a collision. For emergency braking, you have to:

    A. Push as hard as you can on the brake pedal and keep it there.

    B. Apply regulated braking or stab braking.

    C. Use the trailer brakes only.

12. If you want to combine your combination vehicle with a second trailer, protect it by using:

A. Spring brakes in the trailer and emergency air brakes.

B. Chocks on wheels.

C. Either, if available, of the above.

13. How would you be sure that the second trailer was filled with air?

A. Go to the second trailer's rear and open the shut-off emergency line.

B. Watch the air gauge of each trailer for a 30-psi drop.

C. At ten mph, apply the hand valve. You're expected to stop at the same distance as a truck at five mph with one trailer.

14. What is likely to occur if the pintle hook is unlocked when the second trailer is still under the dolly?

A. Air lines are going to rupture.

B. The dolly tow bar would be able to fly up.

C. Nothing can happen until the rig rolls forward.

15. Converter dollies:

A. Often, spring brakes are not available.

B. Since they are small, they have little braking power.

C. A glad-hand converter is typically required.

16. You want your combination to be hooked up to a second trailer with no spring brakes. To do this without wheel chocks, you should:

A. Using the tractor to supply air to the trailer air system and then cut the emergency line.

B. Make sure the trailer rolls freely during the coupling process.

C. Hook the electric cord from the trailer to a portable braking generator.

17. You want to turn right from one two-lane, two-way street to another. The truck is too long to turn without swinging big. You have to move as it shows in:

  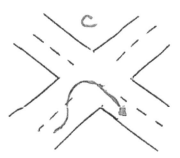

A. Illustration A.

B. Illustration B.

C. Illustration C.

18. Which of these statements is true about controlling the sides' space?

   A. Always keep your car on the right side of the road.

   B. For doubles and triples, high winds are not a concern.

   C. Whenever possible, you should avoid traveling alongside others.

19. To stop all the skids, the safest way is to:

   A. Restore the tires' traction.

   B. Stab or regulated braking is used.

   C. Counter-steer and speed up.

20. Convex or "spot" mirrors are available in certain big trucks. Such mirrors:

   A. Are against the rules in most states.

   B. Make things look smaller than they are and farther away.

   C. As they show a larger area, they do not need to be checked as often as flat mirrors.

21. It takes a driver to drive a truck with double or triple trailers to:

   A. Enable more distances to follow than those for smaller vehicles.

   B. Take extra caution in poor weather and mountain conditions.

   C. Do both of this stuff.

22. Most definitely, the crack-the-whip effect that troubles trucks with trailers will tip over:

   A. A triple rear trailer.

   B. A double rear trailer.

   C. A full trailer behind a truck.

23. The coupling of a converter dolly to the rear trailer is tested visually. How much space should there be between the top and bottom of the fifth wheel?

   A. Depend on the load.

   B. None.

   C. Half an inch to three-quarters of an inch.

24. You drive a set of doubles. A set of wheels for trailers goes into a skid. Which one of these is most likely to take place?

   A. No matter how often the steering wheel twists, the rig will continue to drive in a straight line.

130

B. In a straight line, the rig will remain but slip sideways.

C. You'll jackknife the trailer.

25. You are doing a double or triple trailer rig walk-around inspection. The converter dolly air tank drain valves should be sure and the pintle hook:

A. Open, free.

B. Latched, close.

C. Latched, open.

TRANSPORTING PASSENGER PRACTICE TEST

Directions: All CDL applicants seeking to receive a Transportation Passenger endorsement must take this exam.

1. Buses can have tires that are recapped or re-grooved:

    A. On any of the wheels or both of them.

    B. Only when the speed is less than 40 mph on average.

    C. On the front wheels only.

    D. Everywhere except the front wheels.

2. If a passenger wants to bring a car battery or a can of gasoline or kerosene aboard your bus, you should:

    A. Not allow them to do it.

    B. Tell them they must go to the rear of the bus.

    C. Instruct them to sit next to an open window.

    D. Have the passenger pay a second fare.

3. Which of the following types of emergency equipment must you have on your bus?

    A. Reflectors, fire extinguisher, accident reporting kit.

    B. Fire extinguisher, hydraulic jack, signal flares.

    C. Spare electric fuses, fire extinguisher, reflectors.

    D. Fire extinguisher, accident reporting kit, spare electric fuses.

4. You must not allow the passenger to stand:

    A. Between the wheel wells.

    B. In front of the standee line.

C. Within two feet of an emergency exit.

D. Within two feet of any window.

5. Your bus is disabled. The bus, with passengers aboard, may be towed or pushed to a safe place only:

   A. By another bus with its four-way flashers on.

   B. By a 27,000 GVWR or larger tow truck.

   C. If the distance is less than 500 yards.

   D. If getting off the bus would be riskier for the passengers.

6. When inspecting your bus, you must make sure that:

   A. Every handhold and railing is secure.

   B. Passenger signaling devices are working.

   C. Emergency exit handles are secure.

   D. All of the above.

7. When is it best to wear your seat belt?

   A. Only when you will be driving over 35 mph.

   B. Only if required by company policy.

   C. Only if your bus holds more than 27 people.

   D. Always.

8. Which of these statements about speed management and braking is true?

   A. Stopping time increases one second for each ten mph over 20 mph.

   B. You need about four times as much stopping distance at 40 mph as at 20 mph.

   C. The bus's total stopping distance is the distance it takes to stop once the brakes are put on.

   D. The posted speed limit will always allow you to stop safely.

9. With passengers on board, you must never fuel your bus:

   A. With a higher grade of fuel.

   B. In a closed building.

   C. Without a static chain.

   D. With any of the windows open.

10. When stopping for railroad tracks, you must stop no closer than _____ feet before the nearest track.

   A. Five.

B. Ten.

C. 15.

D. 20.

11. You may sometimes haul small-arms ammunition, emergency shipments of drugs, or hospital supplies on a bus. The total weight of all such hazardous material must not be greater than:

    A. 100 pounds.

    B. 250 pounds.

    C. 500 pounds.

    D. 750 pounds.

12. How are many folding aisle seats permitted in a bus that is not carrying farmworkers?

    A. Zero.

    B. Four.

    C. Six.

    D. Eight.

13. If there is no traffic light or attendant. How far from the draw of a drawbridge must you stop?

    A. Five feet.

    B. Ten feet.

    C. 50 feet.

    D. 100 feet.

14. A bus may carry baggage or freight in the passenger area only if it is secured and meets the following requirements:

    A. The driver can move freely and easily.

    B. Any passenger can use all exits.

    C. Passengers are protected from falling of shifting packages.

    D. All of the above.

15. If your bus is equipped with an emergency exit door, it must:

    A. Be secured when the bus is being driven.

    B. Always have a red door light turned on.

    C. Not have any signs, stickers, or marking near it.

    D. All of the above.

16. Which one of the following types of cargo must never be carried on a bus with a passenger?

    A. Small arms ammunition (ORM-D).

    B. Tear gas.

    C. Emergency hospital supplies.

    D. Emergency drug shipments.

17. When you discharge an unruly passenger, you must choose a place that is:

    A. Off the regular route.

    B. Dark and poorly lighted.

    C. As safe as possible, or the next stop.

    D. The most convenient.

18. When should you check your mirrors for a lane change?

    A. Before and after signaling the change.

    B. Right after starting the lane change.

    C. After completing the lane change.

    D. All of the above.

19. The reason you must be alert for road hazard is so:

    A. Accident reports will be accurate.

    B. Law enforcement personnel can be called.

    C. You will have time to plan your escape if the hazard becomes an emergency.

    D. You can help impaired drivers.

20. How many seats may be placed in the aisle if the bus is a charter and is carrying agricultural (farm) workers?

    A. Zero.

    B. Eight.

    C. Six.

    D. Four.

ANSWERS KEY

21.1. Answer Key for General Knowledge Practice Test

1.B	2.B	3.B	4.B	5.C	6.C	7.A	8.B
9.A	10.B	11.A	12.A	13.B	14.C	15.C	16.A
17.A	18.B	19.A	20.A	21.C	22.B	23.C	24.A
25.A	26.A	27.B	28.C	29.A	30.A	31.B	32.C
33.B	34.B	35.B	36.C	37.B	38.A	39.B	40.A
41.B	42.C	43.A	44.A	45.C	46.A	47.C	48.A
49.A	50.C	51.A	52.A	53.B	54.C	55.C	56.C
57.B	58.A	59.A	60.A	61.A	62.C	63.C	64.C
65.A	66.B	67.B	68.B	69.A	70.A	71.B	72.C
73.A	74.C	75.C	76.B	77.A	78.B	79.C	80.B
81.B	82.C	83.C	84.A	85.B	86.A	87.B	88.A
89.B	90.B	91.C	92.A	93.A	94.C	95.C	96.A
97.C	98.A	99.C	100.A				

21.2. Answer Key for Air Brakes Practice Test

1.B	2.A	3.A	4.A	5.C	6.C	7.B	8.B
9.B	10.A	11.B	12.C	13.A	14.A	15.C	16.C
17.B	18.A	19.B	20.A	21.A	22.A	23.C	24.B
25.B	26.C	27.A	28.C	29.B	30.C		

21.3. Answer Key for Combination Vehicles Practice Test

1.A	2.B	3.A	4.B	5.B	6.B	7.C	8.B
9.B	10.C	11.B	12.C	13.B	14.A	15.C	16.C
17.B	18.C	19.B	20.B	21.B	22.C	23.B	24.A
25.B	26.C	27.C	28.A	29.B	30.A	31.B	32.A

21.4. Answer Key for Hazardous Materials Practice Test

1.C	2.B	3.B	4.A	5.B	6.B	7.C	8.C
9.B	10.C	11.B	12.B	13.A	14.A	15.C	16.B
17.C	18.A	19.B	20.A	21.C	22.A	23.B	24.C
25.C	26.B	27.C	28.A	29.A	30.B	31.A	32.C
33.B	34.C	35.B	36.A	37.A	38.B	39.C	40.A
41.A	42.B	43.B	44.C	45.A	46.C	47.C	48.A
49.B	50.A						

21.5. Answer Key for CDL Tank Vehicles Test

1.C	2.B	3.C	4.B	5.A	6.C	7.A	8.B
9.C	10.B	11.C	12.C	13.A	14.A	15.B	16.A
17.B	18.C	19.C	20.C	21.C	22.A	23.C	24.B
25.C							

21.6. Answer Key for Doubles/Triples Practice Test

1.A	2.A	3.C	4.B	5.B	6.A	7.B	8.A
9.C	10.A	11.B	12.A	13.B	14.B	15.C	16.B
17.C	18.C	19.A	20.B	21.C	22.A	23.C	24.B
25.C							

21.7. Answer Key for Transporting Passenger Practice Test

1.D	2.A	3.D	4.B	5.D	6.D	7.D	8.B
9.C	10.B	11.B	12.A	13.C	14.A	15.A	16.B
17.C	18.A	19.C	20.B				

CDL WRITTEN EXAMINATION GENERAL KNOWLEDGE KEY FACTS

1. One spring leaf, broken or missing, is enough to make it dangerous for a vehicle.

2. There should not be oil, grease, or brake fluid on the brake shoes or pads.

3. Three types of vehicle inspections, pre-trip, en route, and after-trip, are available.

4. Mechanical damage is caused by rough acceleration.

5. Use mirrors to check the tire, other traffic, and the trailer in turns when merging.

6. If exhaust leaks or steering fluid leaks are present, they should be corrected before driving.

7. En route inspected items should include tires, brakes, and securement of cargo.

8. Backing is always dangerous, if possible, should be done towards the side of the drivers and a helper used.

9. If one-fourth of the spring leaves are broken, the vehicle is not allowed to drive.

10. The incorrect size of the tire should not be used on the same vehicle.

11. If the truck uses them, required emergency equipment includes fire extinguishers, warning devices, and spare electrical fuses.

12. The same vehicle should not be fitted with radial and bias-ply tires.

13. Inspection under the hood involves the level of oil, the condition of belts and hoses, and electrical wiring that has been damaged.

138

14. No more than ten degrees of play is allowed on steering wheels.

15. Keep the vehicle from rolling back with the parking brake when starting on an uphill step.

16. Keep in mind that there are blind spots that a mirror cannot show.

17. On opposite sides, keep both hands on your steering wheel.

18. It is appropriate to use turn signals early.

19. On a four split lane highway, warning devices are positioned ten feet, 100 feet, and 200 feet to the rear.

20. Retarders are responsible for slowing the vehicle down and reducing brake wear.

21. The length of a football field requires a heavy vehicle going 55 mph on dry pavement to stop.

22. If traction is poor, skidding can be caused by a retarder.

23. Shift the rear warning device back if a hill or curve prevents other drivers from seeing you from 500 feet behind when you break down.

24. Slow down gradually on slippery roads or stop as quickly as is safe, if on ice.

25. Tap your horn when passing, assume that the other driver is not seeing you, and drive to avoid a crash.

26. To help with shifting and double-clutching, tachometers can be used.

27. The heavier a vehicle is, the faster it goes, and the greater the distance from the stop.

28. Shift down before entering the curves.

29. When setting up warning devices, keep them between you and traffic.

30. At any speed, hydroplaning can occur. With a thin tire tread or low air pressure, this is more likely.

31. Whenever visibility is reduced, headlights should be on.

32. Use the horn only when necessary, so other drivers are startled.

33. 12 to 15 seconds ahead or about a quarter-mile should be looked at by a driver.

34. When you have to slow or stop for something in advance, you should flash your brake lights to warn others.

35. If there are two lanes on the left turn, use the lane on the right turn.

36. Check the tires every two hours or 100 miles while driving in cold weather.

37. Check the tires every 100 miles or two hours while driving in hot weather.

38. Speed decreases by one third on wet roads and one half on snow.

39. Never get a hot radiator cap removed.

40. The height of a vehicle moves with its weight.

41. It is best, if not at an illegal pace, to travel at the same pace as traffic while in traffic.

42. High beams can be used to do so when it is secure and legal.

43. You should raise the following gap when being tailgated.

44. It takes longer to stop on slippery roads, and it is harder to turn without skidding, so turn and slow down as softly as you can.

45. Apply gentle brake pressure to dry the brakes for a short distance while driving.

46. Remember, while entering or crossing traffic, how wide a gap is needed for a heavy vehicle.

47. Be extra cautious about the oil level, fan belt tightness, and avoid high speeds in hot weather.

48. When you turn right from one street with two lanes to another street with two lanes, swing wide after you enter the intersection.

49. Start turning halfway through the intersection while turning left from a two-lane street to another two-lane street.

50. A 40-foot vehicle requires four seconds of space, under good conditions, between it and the vehicle ahead at 35 mph.

51. At night, drive slow enough to stop inside your headlight range.

52. Steer to the right if an oncoming driver drifts into your path.

53. Generally, brake fade is activated by hot brakes.

54. Escape ramps are designed for vehicle harm prevention.

55. Controlled braking is used to hold a vehicle in a straight line.

56. To stop an emergency, counter-steering turns the wheel back in the other direction after steering.

57. Turn no more than is needed to clarify what's in your way when steering to prevent a crash, and do not apply the brakes when turning.

58. A red triangle with an orange center marks a vehicle that is going slowly.

59. Slow down, use your flashers, and alert drivers behind you with your brake lights while driving in work zones.

60. You cannot steer the car if the wheels are skidding while braking.

61. In a gear lower than they arrived, newer trucks can go down long downhill grades.

62. Slow down before the curve when using a curved downhill exit ramp.

63. Avoid braking if you leave the road until the speed is below 20 mph.

64. Try to stop before you get back on the highway if you run on your left shoulder.

65. You can almost always turn faster in case of an emergency than you can pause.

66. Keep the injured warm at an accident scene, avoid heavy bleeding, move them if there is a danger of fire or moving traffic. Don't give the first aid you don't deserve to give.

67. If a pneumatic tire blows out, hold the brake off until it slows down.

68. An electric fire or gasoline fire cannot be put out by water.

69. Pump the lever to try to get the pressure back up if the brake pedal goes to the floor with hydraulic brakes.

70. Under-inflated tires, loose fuel links, or electric shorts may initiate truck fires.

71. On electrical flames, burning liquids, and burning cloth, A, B, C fire extinguishers may be used.

72. If turned abruptly, over-accelerated, or there is an insufficient weight on the front axle, a vehicle will skid.

73. In a front-wheel skid, even though the wheels are rotated, a car appears to drive directly.

74. Release the throttle if the rear wheels slip during acceleration.

75. By stopping the braking, turning rapidly, and counter-steering if needed, a drive wheel braking skid can be fixed.

COMBINATION VEHICLES TEST KEY FACTS

1. Service blue and emergency red are color-coded air lines.

2. Before you back up under a trailer, always verify that the trailer brakes are locked.

3. To help avoid a rollover, load cargo as close to the ground as you can and go slowly around turns.

4. To avoid steering issues, a fifth wheel needs to be kept greased.

5. During normal driving, you cannot use the hand valve to stop a jackknife.

6. You can pull the trailer if you cross the air lines on an old trailer without spring brakes, but you will not have any trailer brakes.

7. When a service air line breaks or comes off before the brakes are applied, normally nothing happens.

8. Never use the hand valve as a brake for parking.

9. It takes longer than a loaded combination vehicle to stop a tractor bobtailing.

10. Glad-hands hooked together can carrying water and soil from the air lines to dummy couplers.

11. The height is right if the trailer only rises slightly to hook when backing under a trailer.

12. There are no spring brakes on many trailers created before 1975.

13. Only to test trailer brakes should hand valves be used.

14. The trailer air supply valve provides the trailer air tanks with air.

15. The tractor safety valve will close and allow the trailer brakes to come on by breaking an emergency air line or both air lines.

16. Often, line up straight before backing under in front of a trailer.

17. Make sure the trailer brakes are working by applying and releasing them.

18. Around the kingpin shank, fifth wheel jaws can still close.

19. The coupling is bad and must be corrected if the fifth wheel locking lever does not lock.

20. For a proper coupling, the fifth wheel safety catch has to be over the locking lever.

21. Before backing up under a trailer, trailer air lines must be connected.

22. Pull gently on the kingpin after hooking, with the trailer brakes closed.

23. The landing gear and its props must clear the frame of the tractor.

24. Set the trailer brakes again after pressurizing the trailer air tanks before backing them under the trailer.

25. There should be no gap between the fifth wheel at the top and bottom.

26. It is often necessary to lift the trailer supports or dollies completely and lock the crank handle before moving.

27. Between the tractor tires and the nose of the trailer, there must be adequate clearance.

28. Wait until the air system is at normal pressure before moving the tractor after pushing in the trailer supply valve.

29. The coupling of combination units is often visually copied.

AIR BRAKE KNOWLEDGE KEY FACTS

1. The brake pedal determines how much air is provided for the brakes to be placed on.

2. S-cam brakes are the most common kind of foundation brakes on heavy vehicles.

3. All vehicles with air brakes must have a pressure gauge for the air supply.

4. Three systems incorporate modern air brake systems. They are the systems for operation, parking, and emergency braking.

5. You can come to a safe stop if a low air pressure device comes on, and proceed only when the machine has been reset.

6. The brake pedal is applied, and the service brakes are released.

7. Spring brakes depend on the adjustment of the service brakes.

8. Air pressure from a separate tank can be used on vehicles with dual parking control valves to release the emergency and or parking brakes to travel a short distance.

9. When air is pumped into the air tanks, the air compressor governor controls it.

10. How much air is applied to the brakes is shown by an application pressure gauge.

11. The air supply gauge shows the amount of air in the air tanks.

12. Air pressure holds back the spring brakes during normal driving.

13. Air tanks with manual drains must be emptied at the end of each day.

14. In the air brake system, water can freeze, causing brake failure.

15. An alcohol evaporator minimizes the risk of ice in the air brake valves.

16. Alcohol evaporators should be tested and filled to the correct amount every day during cold weather.

17. Mechanical pressure, such as spring pressure, must keep the parking or emergency brakes in place.

18. In a straight truck or bus with the motor off and the brakes released, at a pace greater than two psi per minute, the air brake system does not leak. For combination vehicles, apply one psi.

19. On a straight truck or bus with the engine off and brakes applied, at a pace higher than three psi per minute, the air brake system does not leak. For combination vehicles, apply one psi.

20. For the emergency stab braking, pushes as hard as you can on the brake pedal, releasing when the wheels lock up and placing the brakes completely back on when the wheels begin to roll again.

21. Using air brakes takes longer since it takes more time for the air to flow through the lines than hydraulic fluid does.

22. Park on level ground, chock the wheels and release the parking brakes while examining the free play of slack adjusters.

23. Before the air pressure in the service air tank drops below 60 psi, a driver must be able to see a low air pressure warning system coming on.

24. Owing to brake lag, the total stopping time for air brakes is longer.

25. For vehicles fitted with air brakes, parking brakes must be used while the car is parked. This is regardless of whether or not the car is occupied.

26. When it takes tougher brake pressure to manage your speed on a downgrade, your brakes fade.

27. You should not have a delayed stopping motion, any odd sensation, or a pull to one side while checking the service brakes.

28. Brake so that you can steer and keep your car in a straight line while making an emergency stop.

29. Using a low gear and light, steady pedal pressure, the brake linings can stay cooler and help keep the vehicles on long downhill grades at a constant pace.

30. You must stop and park safely as soon as possible when a low-pressure warning system comes on.

TANK ENDORSEMENT KEY FACTS

1. At the posted velocity limit for curves, tankers will turn over. Take curves well below the speeds reported.

2. Because of sanitary requirements, tankers carrying food items are typically "smooth-bore."

3. Baffled tanks have holes to help manage the surge in the internal bulkheads.

4. You must remember the "outage," liquid weight, and permissible limits of weight when loading dense liquids.

5. With "smooth-bore" tanks, especially when stopping and starting, extreme caution must be used.

6. Owing to the elevated center of gravity and liquid flow, tanks need special skills.

7. The flow of liquid in a partially filled cargo tank is a liquid surge.

8. Bulkheads separate a large cargo tank into smaller tanks. Caution must be taken with weight distribution while loading or unloading tanks with bulkheads.

9. The "outage" is the room that must be left when loading a tank to contain the liquid expansion when they warm.

10. In particular, liquid tanks are easy to roll over.

11. When transporting liquids in bulk, the drivers must know the "outage" required.

12. The surge will drive a stopped tank out into an intersection on a slippery surface.

13. Side-to-side surge, especially on curves, can still roll a baffled tank.

14. Unbaffled tanks are referred to as "smooth-bore" tanks and have no surge power at all.

HAZARDOUS MATERIALS
KEY FACTS

1. The shippers must prepare the shipping documents, correctly mark, and properly package a shipment of dangerous materials.

2. The hazardous regulations aim to ensure, communicate the danger, and contain the material for safe drivers and equipment.

3. A vehicle placarded with flammables, oxidizers, or explosives, or while this vehicle is being filled or unloaded, shall not be permitted to smoke within 25 feet.

4. If a car is loaded with explosives and is involved with another car in a collision, the vehicles cannot be pulled apart until the vehicles and inhabited buildings have been positioned 200 feet away from the explosives.

5. A danger class name, hazardous materials shipping name, or ID are not permitted to be used for the description of the non-hazardous material.

6. In the Hazardous Materials Table and Hazardous Substances and Reportable Amounts, the list of hazardous material is found.

7. Do not park a car within 300 feet of a fire containing dangerous materials.

8. The placards must be on all four sides if a vehicle has sufficiently unsafe materials to warrant a placard.

9. Placarded dual tire vehicles must be tested every two hours or 100 miles, whichever is less.

10. If it has an X or an RQ in the HM column of a shipping document, the material displayed on that line must then be a material governed by the legislation on dangerous materials.

11. The freight compartment of vehicles carrying explosives might not be fitted with loose floorboards, sharp points, or a heater for the freight.

12. The correct order of the description of hazardous material on a shipping paper is (1) Proper Shipping Name, (2) Hazard Class, and (3) ID Number.

13. Radioactive materials have a total transport index to calculate the spacing of feet, individuals, freight, and compartment partitions to provide the correct amount of power. The total index of transport does not exceed 50.

14. Placarded vehicles must stop no more than 15 feet from railway crossings and no more than 50 feet from them.

15. There must be no further movement of a vehicle leaking hazardous materials than protection allows.

16. Before driving, the driver must decide the special routes to be used or the need for permits.

17. For rail crossings, vehicles carrying any amount of chlorine must stop.

18. In addition to every other hazard class, you must use poison placards when materials are described as a poison inhalation hazard. Small numbers, also.

19. Poisons must not be put into the same vehicle as foodstuffs of human or animal origin.

20. If the driver has abandoned a vehicle containing dangerous goods, the shipping documents must be abandoned in the driver's seat or the driver's door pocket.

21. Drivers carrying explosives of Class A or B shall have:

    A. The shipping documents.
    B. Written instructions for emergencies.
    C. A written route plan.
    D. A copy of part 397 of FMCSR.

22. Except to the nearest safe spot, do not drive with leaking or flat tires.

23. Remove overheated tires and maintain a safe distance from the car.

24. When fueling a placarded engine, there must always be someone in charge of the fuel nozzle.

25. Drivers transporting radioactive material regulated by the route must undergo special training every two years and bear a dated certificate.

26. Placarded vehicles can only go through open fires if they can do so safely without stopping.

27. It is important to load compressed gas cylinders vertically, horizontally, in racks connected to the truck, or in boxes that do not overturn.

28. If the driver leaves a placarded car in another person's possession, that person must be:

    A. Awake and capable of driving the car.

    B. Understand what to do in an emergency.

    C. Stay 100 feet from the vehicle.

    D. Have a definite view of the car.

29. When handling explosives, the use of hooks or other metal tools is prohibited.

30. For vehicles without explosives, flammable liquids, flammable gases, or empty tanks containing flammable liquids or gases, flares, fuses, or warning fires should not be used.

31. Vehicles carrying chlorine in cargo tanks must be fitted with an authorized gas mask and an emergency leak-control kit for dome cover plates and fittings.

32. The UL minimum. The level for a placarded vehicle control unit fire extinguisher is ten BC.

33. It is illegal to transport explosives of Class A or B in triples or doubles if there is a placarded cargo tank in either of the units.

34. The driver must safely move dangerous materials, without delay, and keep shipping documents in the right place.

35. If the term prohibited appears in the column of the Hazardous Materials Table's hazard class, the substance must not be transported.

36. It is never necessary to park explosives A and B within five feet of the roadway.

37. A properly prepared and signed Standard Hazardous Waste Manifest must be carried at all times while transporting hazardous waste.

38. In an emergency with hazardous materials:

    A. Warn others of the hazard.

    B. Hold the individuals away and upwind.

    C. Smoking prevention.

    D. Keep from the open flames.

39. When hazardous materials leak but do not spill, you can get help by driving to the closest place. If required, call emergency services.

40. A placard for explosives A must be used when transporting both explosives A and B.

41. Mark things with an RQ in the case of a leak. It must be reported to the government before or after an object definition.

42. Close all manholes and valves when dangerous materials are transported in a cargo tank and search for leaks before moving the truck.

CDL WRITTEN EXAMINATION DOUBLES/TRIPLES KEY FACTS

1. Pull the hand valve on and open the service line valve at the rear of the last trailer to verify that the service brakes work to get air to the rear trailer. You can hear the air escape from the valve and sense it.

2. The rule is one second per ten feet of vehicle length, for speeds of 40 mph or less, to measure the number of seconds of space required ahead of your truck. You must add one second for speeds above 40 mph.

3. The proper height for the trailer when hooking a converter dolly to a trailer is such that it will only be lifted slightly when the converter dolly is back under it.

4. With the heaviest trailer in front and the lightest in the back, doubles and triples should always be associated.

5. The crack-the-whip effect increases, and the risk of the rear trailer tipping over increases as the number of trailers increases and/or the length of the combination increases. This crack-the-whip effect makes every sudden movement more vulnerable to the last trailer.

6. Spring brakes, emergency brakes, or wheel chocks must be secured to hook up a second or third trailer.

7. Open the emergency line shut-off valve at the rear of the last trailer to check that air is supplied to the rear trailer.

8. The valve at the rear of the first trailer must be open, and the valve at the rear of the second trailer must be closed to deliver air to the second trailer.

9. Never open a pintle hook that is still under the trailer with the converter dolly. They can fly up the two bars.

10. Generally, there are no spring brakes on the converter dollies. Parking brakes rely on the pressure of the air to work.

11. In general, a trailer jackknife can occur if the trailer wheels on a double or triple combination go into a skid.

12. Parking brakes must have air pressure in the trailer air tank to lock this type of parking brakes on trailers without spring brakes.

CDL TEST PREP-TOP TEN STUDY TIPS

Preparing for your upcoming CDL exam requires dealing with a great deal of information. The typical state CDL manual is over 180 pages long and trying to remember all the information can quickly become overwhelming and frustrating. Instead, the best way to prepare for the CDL exam is to study smart. To help you get started, here are some strategies.

- **Understand what's on the test** — Understand the specific areas in which you are being tested and focus only on that material. Do not study the material; you are not looking for confirmations.
- **Focus on the topics that you are weak on** — You probably have a good feel for the information you are having trouble with. If not, pick up some CDL practice tests or flashcards to identify your weak areas.
- **Study smart** — Take a flexible schedule and study only when you are awake. If you study when you are tired, you will not retain as much as you should.

28.1. Use CDL Practice Tests

Effective preparation for the CDL exam is to familiarize yourself with the questions you will be asked on the exam. Our free CDL practice tests will help you familiarize yourself with the types of questions you might be asked on the actual exam. In addition, our practice tests can reveal your weak areas and provide explanations for your incorrect answers. Below are some methods you can use to get the most out of our practice tests:

- Take an "open-book" test by referring to the CDL manual provided by the state for help as needed.
- Fully interpret any questions you get wrong by carefully reading the explanations you receive after completing the test.
- Take timed tests to help you make sure you understand the content.

28.2. Read the Entire Question Carefully

I strongly recommend that you read each question carefully at least twice before looking at the answer choices. This way, you can avoid falling into traps that the exam writers may have intentionally set up to challenge you. Also, be sure to read each answer option twice before selecting your answer. If you go through the question too quickly, it can lead to errors and confusion.

It is also important that you do not overthink a question. Most questions on the CDL exam are simple and trying to read too much into them can lead to unnecessary confusion. Stick to the facts stated in the question and use your knowledge and experience to choose the best answer choice.

28.3. Don't Jump to Conclusions

Be careful of common traps in multiple-choice questions. One such trap is the appearance of a "reasonable" answer choice as the first choice. This may discourage a test taker from considering other options further down the list that may be the "best" answer. It is important to read and evaluate each answer choice carefully before making a selection. Also, there may be cases where more than one answer choice seems correct. However, it is important that you base your choice solely on the information contained in the question and do not make assumptions.

28.4. First Is Better

It is a good idea to stick with your first answer for questions you are unsure about, especially if you have time to check your answers. Unless you find a clear error in your original answer, it is often best to trust your first instinct.

28.5. Time May Be a Factor

It is important that you maintain a steady pace during the CDL exam, even if your state does not impose a time limit. To determine how much time you should allow for each question, divide the total time by the number of questions in that section. For example, if a section contains 30 questions and takes an hour to complete, you should spend about two minutes on each question. To make sure you stay on schedule, you should check your watch periodically after a few questions. It is also advisable not to get stuck on topics you are unsure about. Either skip them and move on, or make a guess and move on to the next question.

28.6. Know & Go

On the CDL exam, start by answering the questions you are sure about and save the questions you are unsure about for later. Do not waste time trying to answer difficult questions. Instead, mark them and move on to the next question. After you have answered all the questions you are sure about, go back to the marked questions and try to answer them from a new perspective. Sometimes other questions can provide clues or information that will help you answer the questions you were unsure about.

28.7. Answer Everything

Remember, there is no penalty for guessing on your state CDL test. There is an answer for every question. So if you come across a question you are not sure about, try to cross out the obviously wrong answers and make an educated guess from the remaining options. Do not think about it too long and move on to the next question. Remember that time management is key.

28.8. Use the Tricks Wisely

In the questions, some hints can help you spot the correct answer. Here are a few things to watch for:

- Beware of the absolutes — Typically, correct responses do not have absolutes such as never, best, always, must, etc.
- Watch for "except" — It is important that you pay attention when you encounter questions that contain the words "except" or "which of the following is NOT valid". You can try to cover these words to make it easier to answer the question by selecting the option that does not belong. Using this technique, you can avoid getting confused and selecting the wrong answer.
- Valid information — Most of the CDL questions are fairly clear, as described before. Usually, the data found in the query is there for a reason—do not ignore it.

28.9. Your Attitude Matters

Approaching the CDL exam with a positive attitude and confidence can have a significant impact on your performance. If you have prepared well, try to stay relaxed and focused during the test. Remember to take deep breaths and stay calm even when you encounter difficult questions. Have confidence in your abilities and believe that you can pass the test. A positive attitude can help you stay motivated and perform better on the exam.

CDL CASE STUDIES

Case Study 1: Jack's Delivery Service

Jack owns a delivery service and operates a fleet of commercial motor vehicles (CMVs). Recently, one of Jack's drivers was involved in an accident while making a delivery. The driver was cited for not wearing a seatbelt and for following too closely behind another vehicle. Upon further investigation, it was discovered that the driver had not undergone proper training on safety rules and regulations for operating a CMV.

To address this issue, Jack implemented a comprehensive training program for all of his drivers. The program included training on seatbelt use, safe following distances, speed limits, distracted driving, and other important safety rules. Jack also established a system for regular vehicle inspections and maintenance, to ensure that all of his vehicles were in good working condition. As a result of these efforts, Jack's delivery service saw a decrease in accidents and an improvement in driver safety.

Case Study 2: Sarah's Transport Company

Sarah is the owner of a transport company that specializes in transporting hazardous materials. Recently, one of Sarah's drivers was involved in an accident while transporting a load of chemicals. The driver was cited for not following proper protocols for transporting hazardous materials and for not having the necessary endorsements on their commercial driver's license (CDL).

To address this issue, Sarah implemented a strict protocol for transporting hazardous materials, which included proper labeling, packaging, and documentation. Sarah also ensured that all of her drivers had the necessary endorsements on their CDLs before transporting any hazardous materials. Additionally, Sarah provided ongoing training and education on the proper handling and transportation of hazardous materials. As a result of these efforts, Sarah's transport company saw an improvement in safety and compliance with regulations for transporting hazardous materials.

Case Study 3: Tom's Trucking Company

Tom's trucking company operates a fleet of combination vehicles, which require special training and endorsements on a commercial driver's license (CDL). Recently, one of Tom's drivers was involved in an accident while operating a combination vehicle. Upon investigation, it was discovered that the driver had not undergone proper training on operating a combination vehicle and did not have the necessary endorsements on their CDL.

To address this issue, Tom implemented a comprehensive training program for all of his drivers who operate combination vehicles. The program included training on how to properly couple and uncouple trailers, how to inspect combination vehicles before each trip, and how to navigate turns and curves while operating a combination vehicle. Tom also made sure that all of his drivers had the necessary endorsements on their CDLs before operating a combination vehicle. As a result of these efforts, Tom's trucking company saw a decrease in accidents and an improvement in driver safety when operating combination vehicles.

Case Study 4: Mark's Moving Company

Mark owns a moving company and operates a fleet of commercial motor vehicles (CMVs). Recently, one of Mark's drivers was involved in an accident while making a delivery. Upon further investigation, it was discovered that the driver had not undergone proper training on safety rules and regulations for operating a CMV.

To address this issue, Mark implemented a comprehensive training program for all of his drivers. The program included training on seatbelt use, safe following distances, speed limits, distracted driving, and other important safety rules. Mark also established a system for regular vehicle inspections and maintenance, to ensure that all of his vehicles were in good working condition. As a result of these efforts, Mark's moving company saw a decrease in accidents and an improvement in driver safety.

Case Study 5: Jill's Construction Company

Jill is the owner of a construction company that operates a fleet of commercial motor vehicles (CMVs). Recently, one of Jill's drivers was involved in an accident while transporting construction equipment. Upon further investigation, it was discovered that the driver had not undergone proper training on safety rules and regulations for operating a CMV.

To address this issue, Jill implemented a comprehensive training program for all of her drivers. The program included training on safe loading and unloading of construction equipment, securement of loads, and other important safety rules. Jill also established a system for regular vehicle inspections and maintenance, to ensure that all of her vehicles were in good working condition. As a result of these efforts, Jill's construction company saw a decrease in accidents and an improvement in driver safety.

Case Study 6: Alex's Waste Management Company

Alex owns a waste management company and operates a fleet of commercial motor vehicles (CMVs). Recently, one of Alex's drivers was involved in an accident while transporting hazardous waste. Upon further investigation, it was discovered that the driver had not undergone proper training on safety rules and regulations for transporting hazardous materials.

To address this issue, Alex implemented a comprehensive training program for all of his drivers. The program included training on proper labeling, packaging, and documentation for transporting hazardous waste, as well as how to respond in the event of an accident or spill. Alex also ensured that all of his drivers had the necessary endorsements on their commercial driver's license (CDL) before transporting any hazardous materials. As a result of these efforts, Alex's waste management company saw an improvement in safety and compliance with regulations for transporting hazardous waste.

Case Study 7: Laura's Bus Company

Laura owns a bus company that provides transportation for schools and other organizations. Recently, one of Laura's drivers was involved in an accident while transporting a group of students. Upon further investigation, it was discovered that the driver had not undergone proper training on safety rules and regulations for transporting passengers.

To address this issue, Laura implemented a comprehensive training program for all of her drivers. The program included training on passenger safety, including how to secure wheelchair-bound passengers, how to respond in the event of an emergency, and how to interact with passengers in a professional and respectful manner. Laura also established a system for regular vehicle inspections and maintenance, to ensure that all of her vehicles were in good working condition. As a result of these efforts, Laura's bus company saw an improvement in safety and passenger satisfaction.

CDL SAFETY RULES FOR COMMERCIAL MOTOR VEHICLE (CMV) DRIVERS

As a commercial motor vehicle (CMV) driver, safety should be your top priority. You are responsible not only for your own safety, but also for protecting other drivers and pedestrians on the road. You should always follow the following safety rules when driving a truck:

1. **Always wear your seat belt:** Wearing a seat belt when driving a truck is required by law. Failure to wear a seat belt can result in serious injury or even death in the event of an accident. Before driving, make sure you and your passengers are wearing seat belts.

2. **Maintain a safe following distance:** Trucks take more time and distance to come to a stop than smaller vehicles. Always keep a safe distance between your vehicle and the vehicle in front of you to avoid sudden stops or unexpected obstacles on the road.

3. **Observe the speed limits:** Trucks are subject to a lower speed limit than other vehicles on the road. It is important that you obey the posted speed limits and adjust your speed to road and weather conditions.

4. **Perform regular vehicle inspections:** Inspect your vehicle before each trip to make sure it is in good condition. Check tires, brakes, lights and other major components. Report any defects or problems to your supervisor or mechanic.

5. **Avoid distracted driving:** Distracted driving is one of the leading causes of accidents on the road. Avoid distractions such as talking on the phone, eating, or other activities that take your attention off the road.

6. **Never drive under the influence of alcohol:** Driving under the influence of drugs or alcohol is illegal and dangerous. Never drive a truck under the influence of drugs or alcohol.

7. Be aware of blind spots: trucks have large blind spots, which can make it difficult to see other vehicles or pedestrians. Always be aware of your blind spot and use caution when changing lanes or making turns.

8. Use **turn signals:** always use your turn signals when changing lanes or turning. This helps other drivers on the road anticipate your actions and avoid accidents.

9. **Pay attention to weather conditions:** Weather conditions can affect your ability to drive safely. Adjust your speed and driving style to weather conditions such as rain, snow or fog.

10. **Take breaks and get plenty of rest:** Fatigue is a common cause of accidents among truck drivers. Take regular breaks to rest, and get adequate sleep before each trip. Adhere to hours-of-service regulations and do not drive beyond the maximum allowable hours.

By following these safety rules, you can help ensure a safe and successful trip as a commercial motor vehicle driver. Remember, safety should always be your top priority.

CONCLUSION

Once you have passed the required knowledge exam(s) and have held a commercial learner's permit for at least 14 days, you can take the CDL skills exams. These exams test three types of skills, including pre-trip inspection, basic vehicle control, and on-road driving. It is important to know that these exams must be taken on the specific type of vehicle for which you are applying for a license.

Vehicle inspection pre-trip — During the pre-trip inspection, you will be evaluated on your ability to identify potential vehicle safety problems and explain how you would correct them. The inspector may ask you to check different parts of the vehicle, such as the brakes, tires, lights, and steering, and explain what you are checking and why it is important. Note that the vehicle used for the pre-trip inspection should not have any components marked or numbered.

Simple control of the vehicle — The skill test will test your ability to control the vehicle, including driving forward and backward and maneuvering within a specified area, such as turning. Examiners may use traffic lines, cones, or other markings to indicate the areas. The examiner will give you instructions on how to perform each control test.

On-road test - The on-road driving test evaluates your ability to drive safely under a variety of traffic conditions. The test includes situations such as turning left and right, crossing railroad tracks, negotiating curves, driving on inclines and declines, and driving on single and multi-lane roads, highways, and intersections. The examiner will give you instructions on where to drive during the test.

Download your free Audiobook Here:

https://payhip.com/b/UR0Vl

or point your smartphone camera´s here!

Made in United States
North Haven, CT
13 May 2023